THE SEASIDE MURDERS

*Also by Jonathan Goodman
and published by Allison & Busby*

The Pleasures of Murder

The Stabbing of George Harry Storrs

The Railway Murders

The Crippen File

THE SEASIDE MURDERS

Edited by
Jonathan Goodman

ALLISON & BUSBY
LONDON · NEW YORK

For Stan and Jeannie Ellin —
least of all because they helped

First published in Great Britain 1985 by
Allison & Busby Limited
6a Noel Street, London W1V 3RB
and distributed in the USA by
Schocken Books Inc.
62 Cooper Square, New York 10003

This collection copyright © Jonathan Goodman 1985
All rights reserved

British Library Cataloguing in Publication Data

Goodman, Jonathan
  The Seaside murders.
  1. Murder — Great Britain — History
  2. Seaside resorts — Great Britain — History
  I. Title
  364.1'523'0941   HV535.G7

ISBN 0-80531-640-5

Photoset in 11/12pt Sabon by
Ann Buchan (Typesetters), Walton-on-Thames, Surrey
Printed and bound in Great Britain by
Billing and Sons Ltd, Worcester

Contents

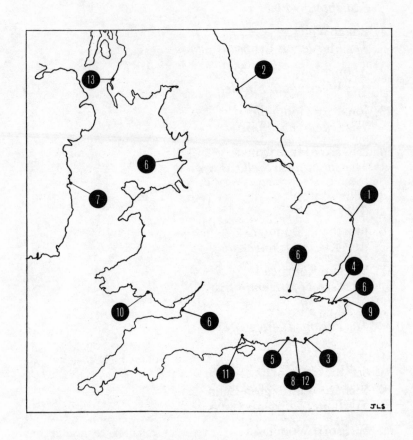

1: Yarmouth, 2: Sunderland, 3: Eastbourne, 4: Whitstable,
5: Shoreham, 6: Weston-super-Mare, Herne Bay,
Blackpool (and North London), 7: Ireland's Eye,
8: Brighton, 9: Margate, 10: Brandy Cove
11: Southampton, 12: Brighton, 13: near Ballantrae

Slaughtering Places

There are several sorts of seaside murder: by and of visitors, by and
· of residents; in places multitudinously favoured for holidays, and in
places that conventional holiday-makers consider last resorts.

Though the sea is beside, or surrounds, all the cases gathered
herein, water plays a murdering part in only two of them, and it is
salty in just one of those. This volume is the third in what was not
planned to be a series. Had the series been premeditated, I should
probably have excluded from *The Pleasures of Murder* (1983) an
account of the killing of Edwin Rose by John Watson Laurie, a fellow
holiday-maker on the Scottish isle of Arran in the summer of 1889—
a case that inspired an anonymous Glaswegian to compose a parody
of a hymn that for a time was sung more frequently in Glasgow, a
very holy city, than was the hymn itself:

> I do believe and shall believe
> That Laurie killed poor Rose,
> And on Goat Fell he shed his blood
> And stole away his clo'es.

And when garnering *The Railway Murders* (1984), I might have
looked for replacements for one or two cases in left-luggage offices of
seaside stations.

An I suppose conspicuous omission from the present collection is
an account of the killing of Francis Rattenbury at his home, the Villa
Madeira, Bournemouth, in 1935. That case is left out because there is
but one decent account of it, that being Fryn Tennyson Jesse's
introduction to *Trial of Alma Victoria Rattenbury and George Percy
Stoner* (William Hodge & Co. Ltd, Edinburgh, 1935; new edition,
1950): it is good that Miss Jesse's piece has been reprinted, without
the benefit of transcript, in several anthologies similar to this one, but
the very fact that there have been so many reprints makes another
unnecessary. I suggest that anyone seeking the essay should, at the
same time, seek Joanna Colenbrander's biography of its author, *A
Portrait of Fryn* (André Deutsch, 1984).

Jonathan Goodman

The Murder
on Yarmouth Sands

Edgar Wallace

The murders committed by criminals who have been classified by criminologists as "Class D Larcenists" make up a very large percentage. It is possible, if one sits in a magistrate's court throughout the year, to collect a list of names which will be almost certain to produce at least one murderer in the course of a generation.

A criminal of this type, however, now and then escapes conviction. He may be wanted by the police, but the chastening experience of prison life, which might possibly bring about a reformation, has been denied to him. He has behind him an embezzlement or two of a petty kind; he has probably been associated with two or three shady methods of obtaining money by false pretences; and to these offences may often be added affairs of gallantry, and, if not a bigamous marriage, at least one marriage and wife-desertion.

There is no more dangerous criminal than a petty larcenist who has escaped the consequences of his offences through, as he believes, his own dexterity and skill. Having this good opinion of himself, he progresses from crime to crime, until there comes a moment when he finds no other escape from the consequences of his meanness and folly than the destruction of a human life which, as he believes, stands between himself and freedom. And so confident is he in his own genius for evasion that he will plan the most diabolical of crimes, perfectly satisfied in his mind that the success which has attended the commission of minor offences will not desert his efforts to evade the penalty of his supreme villainy.

And the meaner the larcenist, the meaner the criminal, the meaner the murder. The greater criminals, the Deemings and the Chapmans, killed on the grand scale. The crimes of such

9

small men as Herbert John Bennett, sometime a labourer at Woolwich Arsenal, are attended by those evidences of low cunning which enabled them to twist a way of escape out of their minor crimes, but which were utterly inadequate to protect them when the more complicated machinery of the law was set in movement, and the brightest brains of Scotland Yard were concentrated against them.

Bennett was a man possessed of a smattering of education he received at one of the elementary schools, and he had, moreover, even as a boy, an ambition to shine in a higher stratum of society than that in which circumstances had placed him. Such ambition is commendable enough, and has brought many a man from the gutter to the highest positions in the land — always providing that the climber has less regard for appearance than for the solid substance of his advancement.

Bennett, by no means intellectual, wished to appear rather than to be; and at the age of sixteen he set himself the task of supplying the deficiencies of his education. He had a mind for dancing, and considered the possibility of being able to play the piano with such skill that he might gain for himself an entry to doors that were now closed to him.

His gropings toward gentility brought him into contact with a young girl, whom he must have regarded as his social superior, since she had many of the attainments which he lacked, and was not only something of a musician, but sufficiently proficient to give lessons on the piano. He was seventeen, she was two years older, and he displayed towards her a devotion which was as passionate as it was ephemeral. Young as he was, he could talk impressively. He left her head reeling with magnificent prospects; the scope of his ambition left her breathless; and when he proposed, as eventually he did, she accepted him. Bennett, despite his youth, was a tempestuous lover.

"He had very big ideas for one of his station. Sometimes he would talk so grandly that even the people who knew him best believed that he was on the point of receiving some exceptionally good appointment, or was about to inherit

enormous sums of money." He had had his smaller
adventures, and fate and an excursion ticket had once carried
him to his first view of the sea — at Yarmouth. At his then
impressionable age, Yarmouth became the first and only
seaside place where happiness was to be found. The Cockney's
devotion to his first love in this respect is proverbial, and there
is little doubt that Yarmouth was, for Bennett, an enchanted
beach ever after, just as Hastings is to the writer, and Brighton
to so many hundreds.

The marriage to the music teacher was a hurried affair. They
appeared one morning before a London registrar, and were
made man and wife. With marriage came disillusionment for
the girl. The great schemes began to dissipate into thin air. The
fine appointment, which would have secured them "a
detached house and garden and possibly some poultry at the
back", did not happen. Bennett made his living by a succession
of little jobs, none of which he retained for any time. He was a
grocer's assistant, a sort of shop-walker; odds and ends of jobs
came his way; his leaving was more or less hurried, and where
there was money to be handled, was accompanied by a
suspicion, amounting in one or two cases to a certainty, that,
in his yearnings for gentility, Bennett had cast overboard the
principle that holds a man to honesty.

He became a canvasser, selling sewing-machines, and his
plausibility and qualities of salesmanship earned him good
commission. There was some suggestion that not all the orders
were genuine, and a possibility that he sold some machines
outright and collected the money for them without accounting
to his employers.

Mrs Bennett had an aged grandmother, with whom the
couple were living. She had a small allowance, sufficient to
keep her, if not in comfort, at least beyond the fear of want.
Her possessions were few, but amongst them was a long silver
chain and a very old-fashioned watch, in which she took great
pride, and to which she attached such importance, though it
was in truth a very clumsy piece of jewellery, that she made one
of those informal, word-of-mouth wills, so common to people
of her class, by saying, "When I am gone, this is yours, my dear."

11

Bennett in Court
A drawing by "Spy" (Leslie Ward)

Eventually she died, and the chain passed to the girl. By that time she was not greatly interested in chains or watches, and even the death of her grandmother brought no very great increase to a burden which was already more than she could bear.

The passionate youth she had married had developed into a bullying, hectoring young man, who never ceased to find fault, who cursed her openly and privately for ruining his life, and who did not hesitate to beat her. A child had been born of the marriage, and while it was coming she had been subjected to every kind of indignity and ill-treatment.

So Bennett moved from job to job. His limited education restricted his opportunities, and there was the additional

Mrs Bennett
(wearing the gold chain)

handicap that he had often to rely upon characters and references which were obviously forged. Of much that would be interesting about this period to the criminologist, there is no trace. It is certain that Bennett was engaged in some nefarious business, for he was changing cheques for large sums, and had suddenly changed his name and became Mr Hood. In this name, he and his wife and baby left, somewhat hurriedly, for South Africa; and it is certain that at the time Bennett had sufficient money, not only to pay the fare out and maintain himself in Cape Town, but also to pay the return fare when, after a very short stay in Cape Town, he decided that South Africa offered no opportunities to a man of his ability, and returned.

Relationships between the Bennetts were now strained. The man had grown tired of his early love, told her she was a millstone about his neck, and attributed the passing of his dreams, the non-fulfilment of the bright promises of his youth, to the handicap of having to provide for her.

Their stay in Cape Town was a matter of days. The newness of the life, or, as he described it, the exclusiveness of Colonial society, irritated and frightened him, and they had scarcely settled down in their lodgings before he was back in the Adderley Street shipping office, arranging his passage back to England.

Their return to London was followed by a separation. He had managed to secure work in Woolwich, and, on the plea that the lodgings they had taken at Bexley Heath were too far from his work, he left his wife and came to live at Woolwich, where he posed as a single man, visiting his wife very occasionally, and doling out to her sufficient money to make both ends meet.

They had taken the lodgings at Bexley Heath in his own name, but it was as Hood that he was best known in Woolwich; and here, free from the encumbrance of his wife, he began to pay attentions to an attractive young girl, Alice Meadows.

Once more he assumed the role of ambitious young man, with immense prospects, and behind him a fascinating experience, for he could now talk of his foreign travels, could speak almost with authority upon South Africa (at that moment a centre of interest, for the Boer War was in progress), and from his imagination could evolve stories of adventure, very fascinating to a young girl who had spent most of her life within the confines of London.

It is clear that Bennett was not depending entirely upon the wages he earned at the Arsenal. He had some other source of revenue, and the probability is that he ran one of his get-rich-quick schemes as a side-line.

In the summer of 1900, soon after Miss Meadows and he had become acquainted, and he had met the Meadows family (impressing them as a young man of singular attainments), the question of a summer holiday was mooted, and what was more natural than that the first place which occurred to him as a likely spot was Yarmouth? At any rate, he wrote to a landlady in the place, asking her if she could reserve rooms for himself and his fiancée. The landlady, if she remembered him at all, was not aware that he was married.

In any case, she had no accommodation at the moment, and accordingly he reserved rooms at a little hotel, and went down with his fiancée, travelling first-class, and spent a week in that delightful pleasure resort. They occupied separate rooms; he was a model of decorum; and those who noticed the rather undistinguished couple observed him as an attentive, considerate young man, who could not do enough for his companion.

The holiday seems to have been of a fairly innocent character. It gave them, however, an opportunity of discussing their future and of fixing the date of their wedding. Bennett, as usual, had great schemes which were on the verge of fruition, and the prospect must indeed have been a very brilliant one to Alice Meadows, who listened, open-mouthed, to the many inventions of her lover, learnt that he was well connected and expected in a very short time to inherit a fine property. Dazzled by his convincing lies, she made preparations to leave the place where she was employed as a domestic servant, and, with the assistance of her family, began to get together the clothes and dainty fripperies which are the especial possessions of a bride.

"A nicely behaved couple — I often saw them strolling along the South Beach," said an observer. "They were a model of what engaged people should be."

But alas for poor Alice Meadows! Her dreams were soon to dissipate into thin air; the growing treasures of clothing she was collecting were never to be worn for his pleasure; and the grand future, so far as he was concerned, was to end dismally on a gallows in Norwich Jail.

It is the failing of all men who worship their own reputations that they must be thought well of at any costs by the person who, for the moment, fills their eye. You may turn the leaves of criminal history and find this queer, perverted vanity showing in every other line. It was the same with Deeming, with Chapman, with Dougal, with Crippen; it is difficult to find a case of murder where this distorted ego does not stand out in the criminal's psychology.

I can recall only three cases, a notable example of which was Smith, the brides-in-the-bath murderer, where this bloated sense of self-importance did not permeate the story of the supreme offence. There is no reason in the world why Bennett should not have married the girl, committing bigamy and risking the consequence of his misdemeanour. There was no reason why Crippen should not have run away with Miss Le Neve, or why Deeming should not have left his wife and children to the charity of his relations. But this passion for making a new start, for wiping out, as they believe, all that is past in one terrible act of savagery, as expressed in sixty per cent of murder cases, was too strong for Herbert Bennett. In his muddled brain there was only one way of establishing himself as a single man and justifying all the lies he had told, and that was by removing the woman who stood between him and a new life.

Probably he also found, at this stage, that the drag upon his financial resources which this double life of his involved was reaching breaking point. He had spent money on holidays, he had given Alice Meadows an engagement ring, and there came from his wife at Bexley Heath a request for a seaside holiday, which gave him the idea which was subsequently carried into effect.

He very seldom met his wife nowadays. His visits to Bexley Heath were few and far between. Nevertheless, his allowance to her enabled her to live without working too hard. She could afford, for example, to send out a small quantity of her linen to a neighbouring laundry.

Bennett does not seem to have been in any dire straits, or to have called upon his wife for assistance to meet his bills. In the course of their married life he had given her four or five rings, and at no time had she been asked to part with these, so the supposition that he had another source of income than his wages at the Arsenal is strengthened; for obviously it would have been impossible for him to have maintained two homes, and carried on an expensive courtship, on his salary as a labourer.

But the end was in sight, and he determined to rid himself of at least one expense; and when his wife mentioned in her letter a wish for a holiday, he replied promptly, suggesting Yarmouth, and giving her the address of the house where, only a month before, he had applied for lodgings for his fiancée.

On this occasion Mrs Rudrum (this was the landlady's name) had a vacancy, and in the beginning of September Mrs Bennett went down to Yarmouth with her child and took up her residence in Mrs Rudrum's house. At her husband's request, however, she changed her name, and it was as Mrs Hood that she was known to her landlady and the very few people who knew her by sight.

A reserved woman, who did not readily make friends, she seemed to be completely satisfied with the companionship of her child. The landlady observed: "The only thing that I noticed about her was that she wore a long silver chain around her neck, and had an old-fashioned watch. She was not the kind of woman that you would notice very much. She was very fond of her little girl and had no other thought than to keep her amused and happy."

One day, when she was strolling along the beach, a beach photographer came to her, and by his professional blandishments induced her to pose for a little tintype picture of herself and the child, and she was all the more ready to agree to his proposition because she had no picture of the little one. And so the photograph was taken, and thereafter occupied a place of honour in her tiny bedroom.

Who she was, and where she came from, nobody knew. Apparently no preliminary letter had been written to the landlady, and until she appeared at Mrs Rudrum's, that lady had no idea she was coming. She was uncommunicative, not inclined to gossip, was typical perhaps of a large number of weekly trippers who visit seaside places, in that she had no identity except as a summer boarder.

Mrs Rudrum was incurious. She did notice, however, that there arrived one morning a letter contained in a bluish-grey envelope and bearing the postmark of Woolwich. The contents of that letter are unknown: the instructions it contained she carried to her grave. But reconstructing the crime in the light of subsequent knowledge, it may be supposed that Bennett wrote to his wife, telling her that he would meet her on the Saturday night, giving her a rendezvous, and in all probability telling her that there was particular reason why he should not be seen in Yarmouth, and also why she should not divulge the fact that he was arriving at all. It is probable, too, that he told her to burn the letter, or else to bring it with her and give it to him when they met; for it is hardly likely that he would take the risk of so incriminating a document being left about for the landlady to see.

She was used to these furtive methods of his. A decent woman, with a respectable life behind her, would not acquiesce in these constant changes of name unless she knew, or believed, that her man's safety depended upon the deception. It is certain, moreover, that she must have been acquainted with his many curious methods of making money, and that she might therefore be dangerous to him if he deserted her.

Something of her complacence and her confidence is traceable to this knowledge. The landlady did not see the letter again, nor did she notice that it had been destroyed, so it is more likely that Bennett insisted upon his wife bringing the letter with her, in order that he could be sure it would fall into no other hands.

On Saturday night she put the child to bed, dressed herself with unusual care, putting on the silver chain and watch, and went out towards the front. She was seen by her landlady walking up and down outside the Town Hall, a building which is very near to the railway station, and it is certain that this was the rendezvous and that she was awaiting for the arrival of the train which would bring Bennett from London.

Coming down, as he did, with murder in his heart, and the

means of encompassing his wife's death in his pocket, and having taken such extraordinary precautions against being associated with the woman, it is almost staggering, yet typical of the careless workings of the criminal mind, that he should not only have met her before the Town Hall, in one of the busiest parts of Yarmouth, but that he should have taken her to a small inn near the quay, where they drank together, afterwards disappearing in the direction of the South Beach.

South Beach at that time was a wild, untended stretch of sand and marram grass, to which courting couples instinctively bent their way. There were innumerable hollows where the swains could be sure of freedom from observation. One such hollow was occupied that night by a man and a girl, who saw two figures come out of the darkness and go into another depression near by. That they were lovers the two observers, very much more interested in themselves than their surroundings, accepted without question.

Bennett, unaware that he had been seen, settled himself down, with his wife at his side, his arm about her, words of love on his lips, and in his hand a mohair boot-lace about nine inches long, with which he intended to commit his hideous crime.

That the deed was done at the very moment when the woman, who still loved him, might expect from him nothing but tenderness, was proved when her body was found. The lovers near by heard a woman's voice pleading for mercy, but thought that the couple were skylarking and took no further notice. While he kissed his wife, Bennett had twisted the lace about her neck, drawn it tight and fastened it with a reef knot. She must have died within a few minutes, whilst he pressed the struggling figure deeper into the sand.

At midnight he appeared at the hotel, where he had stayed only a week or so before with Alice Meadows. His manner was nervous and excited. He told the hotel porter that he had come down by the last train, and that he must leave by the first train out of Yarmouth in the morning. There was no appearance of a struggle; beyond a little agitation and his trembling hands when he took a drink, there was little remarkable in his appearance, and the porter very promptly forgot the incident of the unexpected visitor, called him in the morning in time to catch the seven o'clock train, and thereafter the matter went out of his mind, the more so, as he thought of Bennett as a young man newly engaged and who was, as Bennett had told him on his visit, about to be married to a very charming girl.

So far, we know the story of the murder. We are acquainted not only with the identity but the character of the murderer. We know the circumstances which led Mrs Bennett to adopt the name of Hood, and why she came to Yarmouth. We have to consider now the problem which confronted the police force when, on the Sunday morning, it was reported by an early-morning bather that the dead body of a woman was lying in the sands of South Beach, a mohair lace tied tightly about her neck. Yarmouth was still full of visitors, strangers to the town. It had its quota of undesirables, male and female. The police knew that the South Beach was infested, at certain hours of the night, with queer people, also strangers to the town. When the body was removed to the mortuary, and a brief examination had been made by local and county detectives, there was nothing to reveal who she was, where she had come from, what were the circumstances attending her death.

Their first view was that she was some unfortunate creature who had been maltreated by a chance acquaintance, one of those half-mad murderers who skulk all the time, unsuspected, in our midst. That was the view persisted in for a long time after the inquest jury had returned a verdict.

The first rift in the cloud of anonymity came when Mrs Rudrum, who had learnt of the murder from a neighbour, and who knew that her lodger had not returned all night, came down to the police station and made her report. She was shown the body, and instantly identified her as Mrs Hood. Could the landlady tell the police whether any of her jewellery was missing? The rings were still upon the woman's hands, but the silver chain and the watch had gone.

"What silver chain was that?" asked the chief detective.

Mrs Rudrum tried inadequately to describe the trinket, and then remembered that in the dead woman's room was the little photograph that had been taken on the beach. Accompanied by police officers, she went back to the house, and a very thorough search was made of the room. The photograph was taken away, and every drawer ransacked, for by now the police had learnt of the bluish-grey letter with the Woolwich postmark. But of this there was no trace. Nor was there any other document or writing which could throw the least light upon Mrs Hood's identity, her friends or her place of origin. The landlady knew nothing; her lodger had "kept herself to herself, and told me none of her business".

On some of the linen was a laundry mark — just a number, 599. And with these two most slender of clues, a small tintype picture showing, in microscopic proportions, a blurred chain, and the 599 laundry mark, the police began their search. But at every turn they were baffled. That Mrs Hood had met a man outside the Town Hall, and that she had been seen in a public-house with him only established the suspicion that the murderer was not a chance-found acquaintance, that the woman had met him by appointment, and that he came from somewhere outside of Yarmouth.

The Woolwich postmark narrowed down the search only in so far that every laundry in Woolwich was visited, the marks books inspected, still without bringing the authorities any nearer to their quarry. From time to time the inquest was adjourned, until, after six weeks, it seemed that the case was at an end, and the jury returned a verdict of "Murder against some person or persons unknown".

The photographs were circulated far and wide, but without result for some time. Then, when the search seemed at an end (though such searches are never at an end where the Metropolitan police are concerned), a laundry manageress at Bexley Heath recognized, from the photograph of the laundry mark, the handiwork of her own establishment and, turning up the books, it was discovered that Number 599 had been given to a Mrs Bennett.

The police were at that time systematically exploring every

21

channel that would identify the laundry mark with the murdered woman, and detectives were instantly on the spot. The house in which Mrs Bennett had lived was visited and, without hesitation, a woman who knew her identified, not only the photograph, but the chain which she had been wearing.

At Yarmouth she had told Mrs Rudrum that she was a widow. At Bexley Heath she was known as a married woman, living apart from her husband, and people who lived in the same house remembered that she had frequently received letters which were enclosed in the bluish-grey envelopes that had been described at Yarmouth.

This was only the beginning of the new search. The police might find the sender of the letter, might even discover, as they suspected, that it was the husband of Mrs Hood, and yet unearth no more than a bereaved man, ignorant of his wife's whereabouts and her fate. The investigations in Woolwich began all over again, and finally Herbert Bennett was discovered at the Arsenal.

Bennett had returned to town, and his first act was to meet Alice Meadows in Hyde Park, and subsequently he gave her a number of things belonging to his wife. These, however, did not include the chain and the watch, which he took from his wife's dead body, or, as is more probable, which she handed to him as they were walking along the beach, or when they sat down in the hollow, being afraid of losing something for which she had a personal affection.

Long before any arrest was made, the detectives conducted an inquiry into Bennett's movements. Having established beyond doubt the fact that he was a married man, the further discovery that he was courting another girl and that she was on the threshold of marriage strengthened the suspicion that Bennett was responsible for the death of his wife.

The extraordinary rapidity with which the police work on such occasions as these was facilitated by the fact that Bennett had no idea he was under suspicion, although interrogations had been made of Alice Meadows, his friends had been visited and questioned, and Mrs Bennett's relations had been seen by the police.

During this period Bennett displayed a mild interest in the Yarmouth murder. He had discussed the crime with his wife-to-be and her sister, and had expressed his surprise that the police had not been able to run the murderer to earth. He had even advanced theories as to how the crime was committed and the murderer escaped.

Then, one day, when he might have thought that the crime had blown over, and that the police were now interested in something more promising, two detectives appeared and asked him to accompany them to the police station, and here, to his amazement and horror, he was charged with the murder of his wife.

Bennett then did what so many men have done to tighten the noose about their necks.

"Yarmouth?" he said indignantly. "Why, I have never been to Yarmouth in my life!"

There are so many parallel instances of similar acts of reckless stupidity that we can pass over his extraordinary folly without comment. Not only had he been at Yarmouth, but the police knew that he had been there with Alice Meadows. She herself made no secret of her innocent holiday; and there were the staff at the hotel at which he had stayed to prove the fact beyond any question of doubt.

How slender are the clues on which a murderer's detection hangs! A chance-taken picture made by a beach photographer; the accidental decision of Mrs Bennett to wear her chain on that day — she did not wear it every day — was a link so strong that the cleverest advocate of the day, Mr Marshall Hall, was not able to break it.

Even complete frankness could not have saved Bennett from the scaffold. Had he admitted that he came secretly to see his wife on the night of the murder, and that he left her the next day; if he had admitted his duplicity and the projected act of bigamy; if he had taken the police partly into his confidence; even then that chain which was found in his pormanteau was the most damning proof of his guilt. Without that silver trinket, Bennett could not have been convicted, much less

23

hanged. If, when he found it in his pocket, he had thrown it into the fire, or dropped it into the river, not even his suspicious conduct, his denial of ever having been at Yarmouth, could have brought him to the condemned cell.

But there were the two unchallengeable facts: the silver chain, photographed on the woman two or three days before the murder; the evidence of her landlady that, on the night she went out to meet her husband, she was wearing that chain, and when she was seen outside the Town Hall later in the evening she was still wearing that chain; the absence of the chain from the body when it was discovered; and its finding in his possession — these were the unbreakable chains of proof which he could never shake off. There is an old Spanish saying that every murderer carries in his right hand the proof of his guilt, and never was this proverb so exemplified as in the case of the Yarmouth murder. What malignant imp induced him to take the chain at all, what perversity allowed him to keep it in his possession after the murder was discovered, and long after the description of this trinket had been circulated throughout the kingdom, we cannot tell.

"If the chain had not been found in Bennett's possession," said the greatest criminal authority of the day, "not only would the most striking piece of evidence have been removed from the prosecutor's brief, but there would have actually appeared a point in favour of the prisoner! The disappearance of the chain would have been adduced as a reasonable supposition that Mrs Bennett had been killed by an unknown lover for the sake of its value."

So strong was popular feeling that, instead of being tried at the Norwich Assizes, Bennett was removed to the Old Bailey, and here, before the Lord Chief Justice, Lord Alverston, he made his acquaintance with a London jury. Thirty witnesses were called — witnesses who spoke of Bennett's early married life, of his young wife, and his trip to Yarmouth. There was, of course, no evidence as to any act of felony or misdemeanour which procured him large sums of money from time to time, for the English law does not allow such evidence to be taken when a man is on trial for his life.

There were the hotel porter and the manager, who knew him and had looked after him when he was at Yarmouth with his fiancée. There were the people who saw him in the bar of the little inn near the quay. There was the landlady, and, most distressing of all, the girl to whom he was engaged.

To a man of Bennett's temperament, this was the most uncomfortable witness of all. "It was not the murder he had committed but the lies he had told which upset him," said an observer.

Time and time again we have seen a murderer display the most poignant emotions, not at the recital of his crime, but at the appearance in the witness-box of some person whose opinion he valued, and before whom he must now appear in the light of a boaster and liar.

If it is possible for such a man to possess affection which could be truthfully described as genuine, Bennett had found, in this newest of friends, the love of his life. He had been introduced to her family and had impressed them with his genius and his extraordinary knowledge of affairs. A man of perfect manners, he had impressed that least impressionable of persons, his future wife's sister.

When Alice Meadows stepped into the box, Bennett's eyes dropped; it was the only period during the trial that he gave evidence of his discomfort. Lower and lower sank his head as she related, in that unimpassioned atmosphere, the foolish stories he had told of his career, his prospects, his travels.

Bennett's imagination ran riot when his audience was a woman: his gifts of invention were never so marked as in those circumstances. He could listen without flinching to the record of his horrible deed — more horrible than can be related in cold print; he could watch with a detached interest the display of the trinket which he had taken from his wife a few minutes before her death, and could give his complete attention to the doctor's evidence. To Bennett, that was the least of his embarrassment. The real ordeal for him came when Alice Meadows exposed him as a braggart and a liar.

In this Bennett was not exceptional: all who have attended the trials of great criminals have witnessed a similar phenomenon. Armstrong's averted gaze and discomfort when the evidence of Madame X was being taken, Crippen's agitation when reference was made to his relationship with Miss Le Neve, Seddon's flushed face when the purity of his freemasonry was called into question — one could multiply such instances by a hundred.

Throughout the trial Bennett's behaviour was exemplary.

The trial lasted six days, and at the end the jury required only thirty-five minutes to make up their minds, and, returning to the court, declared Bennett to be guilty of wilful murder. To the very last the man protested his innocence. Even when the judge assumed the black cap he showed neither fear nor any departure from his attitude of a misjudged man.

The sentence of the court was that he should be taken hence, and from thence to Norwich Jail, and that there he should be hanged; and under a strong guard he returned over the familiar route to Norwich — the route he had travelled with Alice Meadows on the way to their holiday; the route he had followed when he was bound for Yarmouth with a cruel murder plan; now to expiate his crime within a few miles of the cemetery where his murdered wife was lying.

Here, on a chill day in March, he met his fate at the hands of the common hangman. But the memory of Bennett will be perpetuated for many years. His conviction will stand as a model of the efficacy of circumstantial evidence. Here was a case where a man committed a murder, and no weapon of any kind was traceable to him — for the mohair lace with which this unfortunate woman was strangled was not identified with one that had been in his possession at any time. There was undoubtedly a motive, though it might be urged that there was no immediate necessity for doing away with his wife, and that he gained very little by his crime. Even the laundry mark was only useful to the police in locating the woman's ordinary place of residence. It was on the flimsy links of an old-fashioned silver chain that the Crown depended to prove that Bennett was the murderer. And most effectively did they succeed.

POSTSCRIPT

From *Murderers' England* by Ivan Butler (London, 1973):

Nearly twelve years later, on Monday, 15 July 1912, an unsolved murder came to light on almost exactly the same spot, though a complete absence of any disturbance of the sand (in contrast to the Bennett case) seemed to suggest that the crime was committed elsewhere and the body brought to the beach later. The victim was eighteen-year-old Dora Grey, who lived with two ladies, Mrs Brooks and Miss Eastick, in a house near the cattle-market. She was an illegitimate child, born in Norwich, and originally taken under the care of Mrs Eastick, mother of the woman she now knew as her "aunt". During the day she worked in a boarding house in Manby Road. On the Sunday before the crime she told a friend she had been to Lowestoft with a "gentleman" and was going to meet him again that evening. She was last seen by a girl-friend, Emily Blythe, walking towards South Beach wearing a big straw hat newly trimmed with roses. Dora Grey was found strangled with a bootlace (as Mary Jane Bennett had been), taken from one of her own shoes. Both shoes and stockings had been removed. Shortly after the murder a large stone was found lying on the spot. On it was written in pencil, "In memory of DORTHY [*sic*] MAUD GREY. May she be revenged. July 15th."

The Wearmouth Murder

Anonymous
(From a *Newgate Calendar*)

A diabolical murder was committed by Jacob Frederick Ehlert, the mate of the Norwegian brigantine *Phoenix*, upon John Berkhalt, captain of the vessel, while she lay in the river at Sunderland. The atrocious transaction was first brought to light by the discovery of the murdered remains of Berkhalt in the river at Sunderland, on Friday, 14 June 1839, with such appearances upon his body as left no doubt that his life had been taken away by violent means; and suspicion at once attached to the crew of his vessel. They were all secured, protesting their ignorance of the murder, and alleging that the captain had gone ashore on the night of the previous Tuesday, since which they had seen nothing of him; but the discovery of marks of blood in his cabin left little doubt of his having been murdered on board the *Phoenix*, and then thrown into the river, in order that his death might be concealed. This belief was speedily confirmed by the confession of a boy named Daniel Frederick Muller, aged nineteen, who was employed in the ship, and who now voluntarily disclosed the whole of the circumstances of the horrible crime, implicating Ehlert, the mate.

His statement was to the following effect:— On the night of Tuesday, 11 June, he had the twelve-o'clock watch, and at about half-past one Ehlert came on deck and called him below. He asked what he was wanted for, but he was desired to ask no questions, but to follow whither he was led. The mate had a hammer and a lantern in his hand, and he went into the captain's cabin. When there he gave the lantern to Muller and desired him to hold it, and then he directly raised his hammer and dealt three tremendous blows on the head of Berkhalt as he lay asleep. The unfortunate man scarcely moved; but

29

Muller, terrified beyond measure, exclaimed, "Mate, what are you doing?" and tried to run away. In this, however, the mate prevented his succeeding, and seizing him by his arm, he said that he must remain. The mate then took the body from the bed and slung a rope round the neck, and he partially clothed it in a pair of stockings and trousers, and then drew a canvas bag over it. The boy now again attempted to escape, but the mate threatened to murder him if he went away, and drew a clasp-knife from his pocket, as if to put his threat into execution; but he told him that if he remained he would give him £300, for there was plenty of money in the captain's cabin. The boy soon after went on deck and wept bitterly, and while he was there the mate came to him and took the skylight off the captain's cabin. He then cut a long cord off the gear, and going below again he tied it round the body, so that he could raise it by that means through the skylight. On his again reaching the deck, he ordered Muller to bring the boat round to the side, and while he was doing so, the boy saw him throw the body over the stern. Both then entered the boat, the mate holding the rope which was attached to the body of the deceased, and they rowed away to the opposite side of the river. The mate there picked up a large stone, and they pulled some distance up against the tide. As they went along, the trousers and bag slipped from the body. At length they stopped, and then the mate, fixing the stone upon the body, let it go, and it sank to the bottom. They now returned to the ship, and Ehlert, having called the next watch, retired to rest; he told the boy that at four o'clock, the conclusion of the present watch, he would call him up as if to take the captain ashore, so that the crew might suppose that he did so. This was done, and he rowed away the boat as if he had the captain in her. The night of the murder was dark and rainy. The boy added that he had done nothing himself in the way of assisting in the murder, but that he had tried very much to get away. The mate had, however, threatened him a great deal so as to prevent his escape, and having compelled him to aid him in the transaction, had given him instructions what to say in the event of his being questioned.

Chine dresses, a blue gabardine costume, a dressing jacket, four cotton blouses, white calico combinations with white lace insertions, a woollen scarf, a nightdress in a case, eight handkerchiefs, three reels of thread, a thimble, a packet of needles, a Bible and two romantic novels.

She set off early on Monday morning, carrying a cheap fibre suitcase and her blue silk handbag. More concerned with looking smart than with wearing clothing appropriate to the season, she wore her Sunday-best coat of green wool with imitation fur twelve inches deep at the bottom and trimming the collar and cuffs.

As soon as she had found somewhere to stay in Eastbourne, she bought half a dozen picture-postcards; one of these she sent to her mother, saying that she had arrived safely and giving her address, and the rest went to friends. To Ada Beasley she wrote:

Seaside, Eastbourne

Dearest Ada. — Arrived here today. Weather is absolutely gorgeous. (Better touch wood.) I'm not in love with Eastbourne yet, but of course I haven't been here a day, so I suppose I cannot really tell you what I think about it. Feeling terribly tired; got up at 5.30 this morning. Suppose you will be going down to Folkestone soon. Please write and let me know. Wish you were down here. Love,

Rene

On Thursday morning Irene received a letter from her mother:

43 Wellington Street,
Portobello,
N.B. [North Britain]

My dear Rennie,

I was so pleased to hear from you. Glad to hear you had got settled, and I hope you will be comfortable. I sent a letter to Manson Place [South Kensington] — I don't know if you got it — telling you I arrived all right. I do wish you had come with me. I am having a good time in a quiet way. Granny was so

35

disappointed at not seeing you. I am being treated awfully well, eating always. They are making such a fuss of me. Such a nice little comfortable cottage, with a small garden at the back, so nice, and everything so spotless and clean. A lovely piano. Mother has it. It is nice to have such comfort. I go up to Aunt Bessie every day. She has a lovely home. They were all so disappointed at not seeing you. Archie is such a nice man. He sent a telegram to you Monday morning to Manson Place. Did you get it? He wanted you to come on by train. He said he would pay your fare. Was it not good of him? Such a nice girl Lizzie, and little Archie. Grandmother has given me a nice dress gold ring for you. I think it would fit you. I have bought a nice sewing machine, a Singer's hand machine. Mother gave it to me, but I am giving her £2 for it as I would not take it for nothing as she had paid £5 15s. for it. It is in perfect order and will be very handy. I have found out now that there is not a boat until the 4th of September. There is one tomorrow and on Friday, and not one until the 4th after that, so I will write to Mrs S. and tell her that I will not be home before that time. Will get home on Sunday evening, the 5th. Aunt Bessie is awfully well off. The house that Granny is in is hers, although she never told me, and this aunt left four houses. She is a lucky one. Uncle Archie has £3 15s. a week and pension 10s. She has had such a lot of jewellery left her, cases of silver spoons and fish knives and forks. You would be surprised to see the beautiful home. Their room is furnished in oak all to match, and a lovely bathroom. The children dressed so nicely. The beach is just close to the house, and there is a lot of shops as it is a small town. I went to the pictures with Aunt Jessie last night as it was raining. Mother has given me a nice warm grey coat for the winter. I think you ought to write to Aunt Bessie. I think I am going to Uncle Robert's in Glasgow on Saturday. The weather is cold here just now. I hope you will be happy at Eastbourne. Tell me all about your lodgings. I think you will manage by yourself for a few days until my return. I hope you will not be too lonely. Get out in the air and mind and keep yourself warm. Put on your coat and have good food. Granny looks very young for her age. She is very active, goes for her own errands. She is a great talker. You would laugh. She is very kind and anxious to make you comfortable. I hope you will make out this scribble. Write and let me know all news. I am now going to Auntie Bessie. Lizzie plays the piano very well. She has been learning for three years. I will have a lot of luggage when I arrive, but I will book at the station what I cannot carry. Being a Sunday I

Irene Munro

don't want carrying a machine. Well, goodbye, hoping to see you soon. Granny and everyone sends their love to you.

Your loving mother,

F. Munro

Send a long letter.

Irene replied at once:

393 Seaside, Eastbourne
Thursday

Dearest Mother,

I was so pleased to get your letter and am very glad to hear it is so lovely up there. I am writing this on the beach. The weather is simply gorgeous, though very windy in the morning, and I feel much better already.

I had the most awful job to get a room. They were full up everywhere, and after trudging about all day was compelled to take a room at 30s. a week. Terrible price, isn't it? but I couldn't get anything else. Even then they couldn't put me up for Monday night, and I had to stay somewhere else and paid 2s.6d. It is of course a lovely room, looking out to the front, with a piano. It is a pity in a way that you are not here as my room is large enough for two people.

I went to Beachy Head on Tuesday evening and lost myself. I didn't get back until nearly eleven o'clock. Yesterday I went to Pevensey Bay — walked there and back.

I have two pounds fifteen left, have paid £1 deposit on my room, so have still 10s. to pay, also fare back to London, so that really I have only £1.10s. left to pay for my rent and board next week, and the remainder of this week: so please do send me down as much as you can to reach me by Saturday as I shall only stay here for a week and shall try to get something cheaper for next week, and I should not like it to come when I am gone. I get awfully hungry down here. I think it must be the sea air.

The name of this road is just "Seaside". Isn't that funny? It is ever such a long road, and I am a threepenny ride from the station.

Goodbye for the present. Please give my love to Grannie, Aunt Jessie, and everyone.

Your affectionate

Rene

A few hours after posting that letter, Irene Munro was savagely murdered. Her body was found the following day, partially buried on the Crumbles, a lonely stretch of shingle and grass running between Eastbourne and Pevensey Bay. She was fully clothed. Her straw hat was pulled over her battered face and weighted down by stones. There was no sign of her blue silk handbag.

The "Crumbles murder" made front-page news. Several popular newspapers were willing to sacrifice truth to sensation, and the most disgraceful imputations were made against the dead girl: the post-mortem examination revealed that she was not a virgin, therefore she was a whore; as she had had a brief relationship with a Frenchman, it followed that she had had any number of affairs; she had bought a cheap pen-case for someone she called "uncle", and it stood to reason that this man was just one of a string of elderly lovers. Such journalistic sophistry must have tortured Mrs Munro, whose shabby gentility extended to not carrying a sewing machine on a Sunday.

While reporters were suggesting that Irene Munro had been killed by a "London lover" and that her handbag had been stolen for the secrets it contained, the Eastbourne police, assisted by Scotland Yard officers, were collecting information about her movements on the last afternoon of her life.

Several witnesses remembered seeing her in the vicinity of her lodgings between two and three o'clock. She was walking in the direction of the Crumbles in company with two young men, the elder of whom was carrying a yellow stick surmounted by a carving of a dog's head. Soon afterwards they were seen by a Royal Navy stoker called William Putland and his friend Frederick Wells; Putland knew the two men by sight and recalled seeing them with "the girl in the green coat" the day before. "To pass away the time and to see what they would do", Putland and Wells followed the trio as far as the Crumbles. Unfortunately, Wells was a half-hearted voyeur; when the girl and her companions climbed under the fence by the railway line along the Crumbles, he turned back towards Eastbourne. His final memory of the incident was seeing the girl offering the men sweets or fruit from a paper bag. Putland hesitated a few moments by the fence, then, not liking the look of the dog's-head stick, ran to catch up with his friend. The last he saw of the girl, she had picked up a stray sandy kitten and was holding it in her arms and stroking it. She and the two men "seemed to be quite jolly and were talking together".

They were next seen a few minutes later by a gang of

navvies who were sitting in a disused railway carriage that was used as a shelter. While the younger man waited arm in arm with the girl, the other man came to the door of the carriage and dropped the kitten inside. "Here you are, here's a kitten for you," he said. The three walked on towards Pevensey; when they were some distance away, one of the men turned back, waved, and shouted: "Look after the kitten." The railway labourers were the last people to see Irene Munro alive. Her body was discovered 500 yards from the carriage.

The police identified Irene Munro's companions as two local men, Jack Field and William Gray. Although only twenty, Field had several convictions, including one for robbery from his mother; since being discharged from the Royal Navy in February, he had been unemployed. Gray, who was twenty-eight, had been born in South Africa of Scottish parents; he had come to England in 1916 with the South African Heavy Artillery and had married an Eastbourne girl, illiterate like himself. He had been out of work for twelve months, spending his small service pension on beer and cigarettes, and relying on his wife's earnings as a domestic servant to keep their home going. Gray had no criminal record, but this was only because his luck had held out; among other offences, he had committed rape and had stolen a purse from a girl, afterwards threatening to "do her in" if she informed the police.

Field and Gray were tried for murder at Lewes Assizes in December. Their answer to the charge was a ramshackle alibi, easily disproved by the police.

While they were waiting to go up the steps to the dock for the verdict, Gray was heard to say to Field: "I never thought we were going to be in this hole." Field replied: "On Irene Munro's coffin were the words 'Thy will be done'."

The jury found both men guilty, but added the rider — an extraordinary one, considering the cold-blooded nature of the murder — that they should be recommended to mercy on the ground that "the crime was not premeditated".

Field and Gray appealed, each blaming the other for the murder, but neither the appeal nor the jury's recommendation was effective.

The killers of Irene Munro were carefully put to death on a chill, misty morning in February 1921. Few tears were shed, and there were no demonstrations of protest.

The Shooting at Stella Maris

Edward Marjoribanks, MP

It was not inappropriate that Sir Edward Marshall Hall's last capital case should be before Mr Justice Avory, whose work at the Criminal Bar, like that of the defender himself, dated back over forty years; they had met so often that each must have been familiar with every professional characteristic which the other possessed.

This appearance was for the defence of Alfonso Austin Smith, who was charged with the murder of John Derham. Both the dead man and the prisoner had been at Eton and Cambridge. The prisoner was the grandson of a Canadian millionaire, had been an officer in the Dragoon Guards, and had at one time been master of a very large fortune. He had served bravely throughout the Great War and had married after it a very attractive lady, who had borne him three children. He was devoted to his family. About six months before the tragedy, he met Derham, a married man, and the two men quickly became great friends. His new friend fell in love with his young wife, and this deeply distressed Smith. Man and wife had not definitely decided to separate on 12 August 1926, and Smith was, in fact, staying with his wife at a villa named Stella Maris at Whitstable, on the northern coast of Kent.

But their matrimonial future was still very uncertain; and, on the 12th, Smith sent, in his wife's name, an "urgent" telegram to Derham, asking him to come down to Stella Maris. These three unhappy people dined together at an hotel. They then returned home, and at 11 p.m. a shot was heard. Mrs Smith's young sister went down to the drawing-room and saw Derham holding Smith down on the floor, and hitting him wildly with a revolver. Mrs Smith was trying to pull Derham away, and eventually he desisted, staggered out of the house, and collapsed in the street. He was mortally wounded, a bullet having entered his left side and come to rest in the right side of his stomach. Two bottles of beer were on the table, and playing-cards were scattered all over the room; altogether the disordered scene was worthy of the pencil of a modern Hogarth.

Mr Roland Oliver was briefed by the Crown, and Marshall Hall, with 350 guineas on his brief, motored down to Maidstone one very foggy November morning to conduct his last capital defence. The fog made him late, and he arrived just as the Court was sitting.

Mr Oliver's opening showed that the prisoner had written menacing letters to the new friend, who, in his opinion, was robbing him of his beloved wife; counsel quoted a letter written that summer to his wife: "My dear, dear Girl, — This problem can only be solved in one way, the removal of your lover Derham or myself. . . . May God forgive me for what I am about to do, and may he forgive you. . . . I have no more to say. My heart is broken and there is nothing in life for me. If you hold anything sacred, in this world or the next, look after the children." To the dead man he had written in July: "You damned swine, I only wish you had the courage to meet me. . . . You must realize that you have ruined, not only a very sweet girl, but the woman I, and not you, love."

All this, however sad and moving to any hearer or reader, seemed to be of little legal assistance to Smith. His defence was shortly expressed in his own words soon after the shooting: "I intended to shoot myself, but in the struggle for the revolver it went off and shot Derham."

If this could be established, the prisoner was guilty neither of murder nor of manslaughter. The chief evidence against the prisoner's account of the matter was that of a passer-by, who said that he heard a shot, and *afterwards* saw Derham and the woman rushing at Smith. But Marshall suggested to him that his mind had subconsciously inverted the sequence of events, there being, at most, only a fraction of a second between the two happenings. The doctor admitted that it was possible for the wound to have been caused while Derham was struggling to seize the revolver, by its barrel, out of the other man's hand, when the latter was in the act of withdrawing it from his hip pocket. The curious place of the wound on the left side might be explained by the twisting of his body in the struggle.

Marshall Hall was very much in his element in this case: he took the big Webley revolver in his hands, and several times he left counsel's benches and went into the well of the court to demonstrate with his old friend Robert Churchill (the gunsmith), the doctor, and even with Mr Roland Oliver himself, in order to show that the wound might easily have been inflicted by an accidental explosion of the revolver as Derham leapt forward to prevent Smith from killing himself. Indeed, Marshall gripped Churchill's wrist with such force that the latter begged him to let go. A discussion took place at some length with Mr Churchill as to the holes which had been made by the bullet in the dead man's clothes. It was sought to fix the range at which the shot had been fired by the nature of the injury to the material. During this discussion Marshall stood with a jeweller's lens in his eye, examining minutely the dead man's clothing which he held in his hands, and testing the gunsmith's evidence with all manner of technical questions.

On the second day the prisoner went into the box. Marshall had handed him the usual alternative form — "I wish to give evidence. I do not wish to give evidence" — but the prisoner wrote back saying that he preferred to put himself unreservedly in the hands of his counsel. Marshall was furious, and explained to Smith that the responsibility was entirely the prisoner's and not the counsel's in this matter, and sent the prisoner a second form. The prisoner struck out the latter part of the alternative, and decided to give evidence. Marshall Hall went over to Smith and said to him, "I feel bound to tell you that I defended a man named Seddon who would have been acquitted, but for his own evidence. He insisted on doing it." But Smith had made up his mind: he was confident that no jury could convict him of murder.

If sympathy had been with the prisoner before, it was far more so after his evidence. He said he had procured the revolver in order to kill himself. The letters which he had written to his wife were read to him. "My Own Adorable Little Wife, — You have made me happier than I ever hoped to be. I have been mad lately and in hell. You asked me to forgive you last night, and I could only say, 'I love you,' and that covered everything. I feel like a man who has been in a terrible fever, delirious and wandering, and am just waking from a deep, refreshing, and life-giving sleep. Do not throw a life-belt to me and then draw it away at my last gasp. You have a great heart and courageous. I need it always and I want it."

"That," asked Sir Edward, "was an honest expression of your feelings to your wife on Wednesday, 11 August 1926?" The prisoner replied, "It is."

Then a most dramatic thing happened: one of the two women on the jury screamed and collapsed, and other women in court began to sob. The woman juror went out and returned in about five minutes, during which time the trial stood adjourned and the prisoner sat waiting in his chair in the witness-box.

Sir Edward then dealt with the agony in the prisoner's mind when he saw that the reconciliation with his wife was not permanent. He went and possessed himself of his revolver.

"What was your state of mind?" asked Sir Edward. — "Impossible to describe."

"The lifebelt had been withdrawn?" — "Yes."

He described how he had sent for Derham so that the three of them could talk the matter over. It was apparently suggested by the other two that Smith should go away.

"Where were you to stay?" asked Sir Edward. "Oh, it didn't matter where I went," replied the prisoner.

He said the tragedy had occurred in a flash, when Derham and his wife were sorting out the cards for a game. He told them he was going to shoot himself. "It did not appear to distress them. They did not believe it."

The prisoner then told and demonstrated how he had felt for the revolver in his hip pocket. "The next thing that happened — all I know is — there was a terrific struggle. I was struck on the head, the revolver went off, and the next thing I was absolutely conscious of was speaking to Inspector Rivers."

His last answer in examination-in-chief was, "I swear I never touched the trigger."

Mr Oliver's first question was a most dramatic one: "Do you think a man who behaved as Derham behaved deserves to be killed?"

The accused replied, "I do not think any man deserves to be killed." This was the key-note of Mr Oliver's very fair cross-examination, and he put to the prisoner other letters written to his wife. "I cannot live without you, nor do I intend to. . . . For the children's sake send him away. Chappie won't want to have fingers pointed at him as the son of the murderer of an unfaithful wife and her lover, and a suicide. Come back to me, my girl, my little white heather." (The prisoner during the trial had worn a little sprig of white heather in his button-hole.) In another letter he wrote of his children, "If only you knew how I long to see you and them. Is it fair that they should have no daddy?"

When the judge questioned him about the possibility of a reconciliation, the prisoner said earnestly, "She had become reconciled the day before. . . . I thought I could even persuade Derham to see the folly of it. . . . Derham was a gentleman. I might have appealed to his better nature."

The prisoner had made a most convincing and moving witness, and, by the time he had left the box, Marshall Hall felt sure that the jury believed his account of what had happened, and would acquit him on his own evidence. But there was still the speech to be made, and, since he had only called the prisoner, Marshall Hall had the last word.

It was a fine speech, a worthy coping stone to his great career, but it is exceedingly scantily reported. "Is it conceivable," he said, "that a man who was going to murder another would manufacture evidence against himself by sending a telegram, drafted in his own handwriting, under his wife's name, and that he would show the reply to the telegram to his wife? Had Smith had any intentions of murdering Derham, he could have done so while walking home from the Marine Hotel. . . . Smith found himself with the only things in the world which he loved and adored, his wife and children, being taken away from him, and he had come to a stage when it seemed wellnigh hopeless to go on under existing conditions. The only solution which appeared to him was to take his own life, but even up to the last he was hoping — desperately, perhaps — for a reconciliation, and deferred the moment till the time when hope was no longer a possibility."

Sir Edward concluded with a passionate appeal to set free a man who had been cruelly buffeted by fate. "He begged his wife not to withdraw the lifebelt, which she had thrown him as he was struggling in the water. That lifebelt had been withdrawn once. Members of the jury, it is now for you to say whether you will throw him that lifebelt once more, give him the chance of grasping it and being pulled ashore to resume his old happy life with the woman he loves, which has been so long denied to him."

Curiously enough, Smith had almost been drowned in the river at Thames Ditton after long and fruitless efforts to rescue a friend, and had only just been pulled ashore in time for his life to be saved.

In his summing-up, the judge observed, "The law you have to administer in this case is the law of this country and not of any other, and, above all, not that which is erroneously called the 'unwritten law'. That is merely a name for no law at all. It is the name given to the proposition that every man and woman is a law unto himself or herself, and that reverts us to a state of barbarism. I have told you the law of this country, and it must be applied. If you apply any other law or notions of your own, you are violating the oaths you have taken."

The jury were out of court for two hours and eleven minutes before they came to their decision. They declared the prisoner not guilty, both of murder and manslaughter. The judge entered the two verdicts; everybody in court thought that he was about to discharge the prisoner; but it was not so.

"There is another charge on the calendar against the prisoner," he said.

It appeared that the prisoner was also charged, under a statute, with "possessing fire-arms and ammunition with intent to endanger life". On his own evidence he had intended

48

to take his own life, and the judge held that the statute applied. The prisoner pleaded "Guilty" to this charge, and he was sentenced to twelve months' imprisonment with hard labour. In this rather unexpected way ended the Stella Maris trial. Once before, Marshall Hall had run, in dangerous combination, provocation and accident; once more he brought them into harmony, and so his last victory was won. He had fought the case with all his usual vigour and vitality. In no single particular did his powers seem to be failing. It was as if he were still in the prime of life.

During his stay at Maidstone, Marshall Hall went over part of Maidstone Gaol, and, while he was passing through one of the workrooms, he suddenly caught sight of a familiar figure, an old client on whose behalf he had appeared for over twenty years. This man had been a member of Parliament and in his way a great national figure. The two men's eyes met for an instant: it would have been unlawful for Marshall Hall to have spoken to a prisoner, but it would also have been impossible for a man of his generous nature not to make some gesture of recognition; he raised his hand to his mouth, blew his old client a kiss, and passed on.

A few days after the Stella Maris trial, Marshall came to lunch with me at a famous London hotel. He could talk of nothing but this case, and we were only too anxious to hear him. It was not very long before he was repeating to us the peroration of his final speech; and when he reached the "lifebelt" passage, Mr J. C. Squire, who was sitting opposite to him, said, quite carried away, "My God, Marshall, that's poetry," while a musical-comedy star of twenty-five summers, who was sitting next to him, whispered to me, "Take this man away — he's breaking my heart". Meanwhile, the waiters had gathered round, and were scandalously neglecting their obligations to other patrons.

EDITOR'S NOTE: *Marshall Hall died on 23 February 1927.*

Angels of Death

Hugh Johnson
(Professor of Forensic Medicine,
St Thomas's Hospital Medical School, London)

It all started on Thursday, 19 April 1973, when the Sussex Police rang me up and asked me to come down to Shoreham Harbour. At eight o'clock that evening, I met Detective Chief Superintendent Marshall and other police officers at the part of Shoreham Harbour known as the Aldrington Basin, where I was shown the body of a well-built man lying at the edge of the jetty. He was fully clothed; there were several turns of rope around his shins and ankles, and an end of the rope was attached to a plastic carrier-bag containing stone blocks. One hand was detached from the body, lying beside it, and the head was skeletonized. What had happened, it seemed, was that a ship manoeuvring in the basin, with its propellers racing, had disturbed the silt at the bottom of the harbour and brought the body to the surface, fortunately without injuring it. I cut the rope attaching the body to the plastic bag, and we took the body to Hove Borough Mortuary, where I began a very extensive post-mortem examination.

The body was that of a young man, approximately six feet in height. The clothing was unremarkable; but on searching it I found in a hip-pocket a folded piece of paper, apparently a receipt from Hove Magistrates Court, and in another pocket a white-metal bracelet with the word "Olly" on the face and "Julie" on the reverse.

I removed all the turns of rope with the knots, taking care to identify the various cut ends so that they could be reconstituted in the Forensic Science Laboratory, and then we removed the clothing, which bore no identification marks.

On the right forearm was a crudely-executed tattoo in the form of a heart with an arrow through it and some lettering, much of which was indecipherable, and there was a further tattoo above this in the form of a letter *H*. I was able to bring up the tattoo by rubbing away the superficial layers of the skin, the epidermis, thus revealing the tattoo in the underlying dermis much more clearly — rather like removing the patina of varnish from an Old Master painting. Presumably the head was skeletonized by the depredations of fish and other marine creatures; the lower jaw was missing, as were several teeth in the upper jaw, but I saw that the wisdom teeth had not erupted, which suggested a probable age of eighteen years or less.

In the course of my examination, I tried to establish a cause of death. There was no sign of any head injury so far as I could see; no fracture of the skull. I identified the various structures in the throat, which were all intact (tending to rule out strangulation), and the bones and structures of the chest were intact. All the air passages contained black debris, and the lungs were sodden with fluid. There was nothing else to find; all the organs were apparently intact, healthy and uninjured. Having removed a very large collection of samples, I handed most of these to the police for laboratory examination, and retained a lung, a kidney, and part of the shaft of the right thigh-bone.

While I had been conducting my examination, the police had been examining the contents of the pockets: particularly the paper from Hove Magistrates Court. The document related to one Clive Edward Jeremy Olive, aged sixteen and a half, who had been reported missing to the police at the end of February 1973. We obtained a physical description of the missing boy, and this seemed to fit that of the body very well.

I returned to London with my specimens, and subsequently arranged for the preparation of extracts from the tissues on microscope slides, with the intention of looking for diatoms. Diatoms are microscopic unicellular algae which are found wherever there is water. There are about 15,000 species known to science; roughly half of these live in fresh water, while the remainder are found in the sea or in brackish water. The species vary from site to site, depending on whether the

Aldrington Basin, 19 April 1973
By permission of the Chief Constable of Sussex

water is hot or cold, running or stagnant, acid or neutral, and so on. When a person dies from drowning, water inhaled into the lungs brings with it any diatoms that are present in the water; these diatoms travel through the circulation in the few minutes it takes a person to die from drowning, and by the time the heart stops and the circulation comes to a standstill, the diatoms are distributed throughout the body. Contrariwise, if a body is dead before it goes into the water, and there is no circulation, diatoms may enter the body through the windpipe or through defects caused by injury — but they will not reach all the deeper and more inaccessible sites (for example, the bone-marrow of the long bones or the kidney). The identification of numerous diatoms through the body of the same species that are present in the water where the body was found is indicative of the fact that the person has died of drowning in that water. Diatoms have silaceous shells which are resistant to acid digestion. What one does is to take portions of tissue (taking care not to contaminate them with water), digest them with strong nitric and sulphuric acid, thus

53

destroying all the organic material, leaving only the silica shells of the diatoms, neutralize the acid, prepare slides of the deposit of the shells, and examine them under the microscope. Of course, as a control one must have a sample of the water from the locus, similarly treated so that the diatoms in it can be identified and compared with those found in the tissues. In the case of Clive Olive, I was able to see numerous diatoms in all the slides which I had prepared, and these corresponded exactly with those in the water of the Aldrington Basin. I was thus able to conclude that Clive Olive had died of drowning, that he had no natural disease to have caused or influenced his death, that he had died in the harbour where he was found, and that there was no obvious significant injury which might have played any part in his death.

Meanwhile, the police were continuing their inquiries. They soon established that Clive, who lived in Hove, had vanished on 28 February. He had had many aliases and had dabbled in drugs — probably only marijuana. He had joined a Brighton Hell's Angels chapter called the Mad Dogs but had fallen out with them and joined a chapter in Hove called the Cougars. He was obviously deeply involved with Hell's Angels; his mother said that "their influence on Clive was far greater than mine, he did exactly as they told him to do; they were evil and horrible, and I did my best to keep him away from them". The police interviewed a very large number of young people in the Hove area, and twelve days after the finding of Clive Olive's body, three persons were charged with his murder. They were a pregnant eighteen-year-old girl named Christine Dorn, her husband Albert, aged twenty-seven, and her twenty-one-year-old brother Brian Moore, all of whom lived in Brighton.

An inquest was opened by Dr Sommerville, the East Sussex Coroner, on 13 June. After formal evidence of identification, I gave the cause of death as drowning and said that the body had no injuries and no natural disease. The whole proceedings lasted only two minutes.

On 12 July the three accused were committed for trial at Lewes Crown Court. The trial opened there on Monday, 26 November, before Mr Justice Thesiger. Mr Michael Eastham,

QC, prosecuting, described the finding of the body and set out the prosecution case that the accused went in Dorn's van, which contained, among other things, rope, concrete blocks and a bag to be used for the disposal of the body, to Shoreham Harbour; there, Moore attacked Olive with his fists and battered him about the head with a truncheon; the body was then bound up and weighted, and Moore and Dorn threw it into the harbour while Mrs Dorn remained in the car.

Mr Eastham said that Olive had known a girl called Jane in 1972 and boasted of his sexual activities with her; but by the autumn of that year Jane had become Moore's girl-friend. Jane told Moore that she had met Olive in September 1972, on her sixteenth birthday, when he had induced her to come back to his mother's flat and had raped her. This information preyed on Moore's mind: he brought up the subject from time to time and told her he would "get" Olive — that he would kill him or at least beat him up. He had apparently told other people: "I know who it is. I am going to get him. I will get him sooner or later." Olive at the time was working as a washer-up in a café called the Gondola. On 27 February, the three accused met Olive, but they did not offer him any violence as they had not brought their impedimenta with them in the van. They told him a story about being able to get drugs for him, and arranged to meet him the following night: Wednesday, 28 February.

Earlier that day, they had stolen concrete blocks, a plastic bag, and rope from two building sites, and placed their haul in the van. They picked up Olive at the Gondola, and Dorn drove the van to Shoreham Harbour, where Moore beat up Olive while Dorn and his wife kept a look-out. Believing Olive to be dead, the two men weighted the body with the blocks in the plastic bag, then threw it into the harbour.

Statements by Moore that were read out in Court described in detail the planning and execution of the killing. After speaking of the purloining of the bag, concrete blocks and rope, he went on: "The reason we took these things was because I thought I might lose my temper when we saw Olly and I thought I might kill him. I decided if I killed him I would tie him up and put him in the harbour. I got the idea off the

Mad Dogs, who were going to kill their leader in the same way. I talked to Olly about Jane. I grabbed him. I went into simple words and I asked him, have you fucked her? I had this truncheon. I lost my temper. I belted him with my fists and I caught him on his face. He started crying, then I knocked him back with my hand and straight afterwards I belted him with a stick a couple of times. He gave an almighty scream, then Olly was out and slumped. . . . I thought he was dead. While Al [Dorn] drove him in the van I started tying him up. I connected the bag to his feet with the bricks in it. We drove straight up to about ten yards from the water in the harbour and turned round and backed up. Al dropped in the bag and I dropped the body. What got Al was the bubbles. What got me was the staring eyes." These facts were more or less corroborated by the other two defendants in their statements.

Jane, a seventeen-year-old schoolgirl at the time of the trial, described how Olive sexually assaulted her and how she had subsequently spoken of the attack to Moore. She told how Moore had met her on the morning of 1 March, the day after the alleged killing, and walked her to school. On the way, they stopped at a café for a cup of tea, and there Moore said that he and the Dorns had killed Olive, and explained how it had taken place. She continued to see Moore until 30 April, the day before he was arrested. She said that they were in a car going to Worthing when they heard on the radio that the body had been found. She described her parents' reaction to Clive Olive when she took him home; her mother had not liked him, and so the visit had not been a success. When she started going out with Moore, life had become much easier as her parents had both liked him. She said: "I found him kind and gentle and extremely loving and very, very protective. It was a happy relationship together until this business about Clive Olive came up between us, when I told him Clive Olive had raped me. He seemed unable thereafter to put it out of his mind. Even when he was not talking about it, he was thinking about it most of the time. It made me unhappy and it certainly made him very unhappy. He wanted to know exactly what had happened. We had a ritual burning of the clothes that I had been wearing at the time. He insisted on re-enacting the scene between me and Clive, not to the extent of having intercourse — it didn't get that far, and it ended up when we both broke down in tears."

I gave evidence about my post-mortem examination and conclusions as to the cause of death. Among other witnesses was a Hell's Angel called Smith who used the nicknames "Rex", "Randy", "Thicker", "Simple" and "Loner"; brought from prison. Mr Smith said that the president of the Mad Dogs was a man called "Wank", "Tramp" was the vice-president, "Bluey" was the secretary, and "Gyp" was the treasurer. The Mad Dogs had a woman member nicknamed "Butch" whom he identified as Christine Dorn. Before Olive became a member, he went through an initiation ceremony on the beach at Brighton which apparently involved the mixing of blood from cut arms over the saddle of a motor-bike. Detective Sergeant Taylor described an interview with Moore in which he said: "I lifted his head up with my truncheon and his eyes were all staring. It was diabolical."

When it was his turn to give evidence, Moore, while describing the events in similar terms to those in his written statements, said to the Court: "I don't feel I have done anything wrong. I knew it was against the law, but what he had done was also against the law, he had raped my girl. Nobody else would do it, so I felt it would be my job." Moore made a striking figure in court, since his long red hair was tied in a pony-tail and he was wearing a bus-conductor's jacket. He admitted having been on drugs, but said he did not need them any more. He told how he had met Jane — "it was love at first sight" — and said that he had been greatly upset when she told him about being raped.

The trial continued until 6 December, when the jury, after a retirement of six and a half hours, found Moore and Dorn guilty of murder, and Mrs Dorn not guilty of murder but guilty of manslaughter. Moore and Dorn were sentenced to life imprisonment; Mrs Dorn to ten years. Mr Justice Thesiger described the case as "one of the most horrible murders", adding: "I feel sure that no one minded a bit whether [Olive] was dead or alive when he was put in the water that night."

Detectives who investigated the case had such difficulty in understanding the obscure language used by Hell's Angels that they had to bring an interpreter to compile a glossary of phrases; this has since been circulated to other police forces. The Mad Dogs of Sussex chapter of Hell's Angels, to which all the persons involved in the case belonged, was only a poor imitation of the real thing. For one thing, hardly any of the members owned motorcycles, a prerequisite of the subculture practised by the movement which started among the youth of California about 1950.

Moore, a drifter, had several convictions for stealing. He had worked for eighteen months at Brighton Aquarium, then at a flamingo park in Yorkshire. He returned to Brighton, quarrelled with the manager of the aquarium over training methods, and pushed him into the pool. At the age of twenty-one, he obtained employment at Windsor Safari Park and was promoted from deputy head keeper to head keeper in a short time. He had a steady girl-friend at that time; after a row with her, he decided to commit suicide by walking into a cage occupied by two leopards, locking the door and throwing the keys outside. The attempt failed because the leopards simply ignored him. Subsequently he turned to drugs, and in 1969 joined the Mad Dogs.

Christine Dorn had been involved with various groups of Hell's Angels. Pregnant at the time of the murder, she gave birth while in custody awaiting trial. When sentenced, she fainted into the arms of a woman prison officer. However, she rapidly recovered and was led away, sobbing and screaming "You bastard" at the judge. Albert Dorn — a rather grey figure, who seemed to have acted under the influence of his brother-in-law — looked more embarrassed than perturbed by the scene.

The following year, Moore and Dorn were refused leave to appeal. But the Court of Appeal reversed the manslaughter conviction against Christine. According to *The Times* of 22 November 1974, Lord Justice Cairns said that Mrs Dorn had been a spectator and nothing more. The jury had acquitted her of murder, but the trial judge had earlier directed them that they could find her guilty of manslaughter if they felt that, believing Clive Olive to be dead, she had encouraged or assisted the others in the disposal of the body. It was clear, said Lord Justice Cairns, that she had not helped in that way.

Also Known as Love

Jonathan Goodman

Consider, friends, George Joseph Smith,
A Briton not to trifle with,
When wives aroused his greed or wrath
He led them firmly to the bath.
Instead of guzzling in the pub,
He drowned his troubles in the tub.

*From "They Don't Read De Quincey in Philly
or Cincy" by Ogden Nash*

Although two hundred miles separate 16 Regent's Road, Blackpool, from 14 Bismarck Road[1] in the North London suburb of Highgate, and sixty miles separate the latter address from 80 High Street, Herne Bay, the three places have a gruesome fact in common — a fact that, with others, came to light early in 1915, capturing the attention of newspaper readers to such an extent that reports concerning hostilities with the Boche were on some days, in some papers, given second billing on the front page.

One supposes that the most avid readers of the accounts of how people had taken a bath but not lived long enough to dry themselves were women, young and not so young, about to embark on matrimony; and their mothers, fearful that, in gaining a son-in-law, they might be losing a daughter for good and all. Perhaps some of the more apprehensive mothers added to their birds-and-bees advice the warning that, at least during the nuptial period, their daughters should forget that cleanliness is next to godliness, and steer clear of bath-tubs.

1 Now called Waterlow Road. During the Great War, all Bismarck-entitled thoroughfares in the capital patriotically were renamed.

61

The man whose activities had caused the maidenly and maternal worries about the cause-and-effect relationship between personal hygiene and sudden death was born in Bethnal Green, a sleazy district of East London, in January 1872. He was christened George Joseph Smith.

The first name was also that of his father, who was an insurance agent. If the father was at all good at his job, presumably he was a slick talker — and if so, then George junior's power to charm the birds was partly inherited. Only partly, though. Considering how, by the time he was in his mid-twenties, he was using — or rather, misusing — women, he must have practised the deceit of blandishment, learning from trial and error, so that an innate talent was disciplined and refined into something akin to genius.

You may sneer at the notion, but I am inclined to believe that Smith's fatal fascination for women (truly fatal, so far as some of his victims were concerned) was in some measure optically induced. According to one of the lady-friends who lived to tell the tale, "He had an extraordinary power. . . . This power lay in his eyes. When he looked at you for a minute or two, you had the feeling that you were being magnetized. They were little eyes that seemed to rob you of your will." Other women said much the same thing. And Edward Marshall Hall, the great barrister, once broke off an interview with Smith because he believed that an attempt was being made to hypnotize him.

But if Smith was a hypnotist, he either developed the skill in manhood or, possessing it earlier, displayed it only as a party-trick during his formative years. Hypnotism, mesmerism, call it what you will, can hardly have played a part in his fledgling criminal schemes, the unsuccessfulness of which might have caused a less dedicated apprentice crook to make the best of some thoroughly bad jobs and seek a licit calling. The final act apart, the story of the life and crimes of George Joseph Smith provides an object lesson to all aspiring villains: If at first you not only don't succeed, but fail abysmally, try to find a novel method of fleecing.

*

By the age of ten, Smith had committed such an assortment of misdemeanours that it was decided that the community — and he, too, perhaps — would be far better off if he were in a reformatory. He was despatched to one at Gravesend (a name that might be considered portentous of his way of breaking off relationships in later life), and there he stayed until he was sixteen. Drawing no righteous morals from the experience, he was no sooner back with his mother — who was now living alone, whether widowed or deserted I cannot be sure — than he was being troublesome again. A small theft was punished by a sentence of seven days' imprisonment. Out again, he took a fancy to a bicycle, and so was soon back in gaol, serving six months with hard labour. He was released in the late summer of 1891.

Perhaps, as he subsequently claimed, he spent the next few years in the army. That might explain why, during that period, no further entries appeared on the police record-sheet headed "SMITH, George Joseph". On the other hand, he may have been more discreet in his criminal activities — or simply fortunate not to be caught. Another possibility is that his transgressions were recorded on record-sheets bearing names other than his own: distinctly likely, this, for when he was arrested for his final, dreadful offences, the list of his aliases looked not unlike an electoral roll for a small town.

He was "George Baker" when, in July 1896, he was sentenced to a year in prison for three cases of larceny and receiving. The fact does not appear to have been included in the evidence against him, but by now he had latched on to the idea of using members of the fair sex unfairly: he had persuaded a domestic servant to become a job-hopper, misappropriating her employers' property shortly before each hop.

The following year, once he was free, he moved to Leicester. As a sort of "in-joke", so esoteric that he allowed no one else to appreciate it, he called himself "Love". Caroline Thornhill, a teenaged native of the lacemaking town, fell under the spell of "Love" — but not to the extent of accepting his suggestion that they should live in sin. So in January 1898, when he was just twenty-six, he married Caroline. The wedding was a quiet affair, for the bride's relatives so disapproved of "George Love" that they boycotted the ceremony.

The relatives were soon able to remind Caroline that they "had told her so". Within six months, life with "Love" became intolerable, and Caroline sought refuge with a cousin in Nottingham. But her husband pursued her; and persuaded her to accompany him south, where — first in London, then farther south, in the seaside towns of Brighton, Hove, and Hastings — he wrote references, posing as her last employer, which helped her to obtain domestic posts. Perhaps needless to say, each house in which she worked was less well stocked with trinkets by the time she moved on to the next position George had chosen for her. The crooks' tour ended when the Hastings police arrested "Mrs Love". Smith managed to evade capture. He travelled to London, booked into a boarding house, and, rather than fork out money for his digs, "married" the landlady at a registry office near Buckingham Palace. That was in 1899.

About a year later, Caroline chanced to spot Smith window-shopping in Oxford Street. She informed a constable. As her husband was led away, she called after him, "Treacle is sweet — but revenge is sweeter". Found guilty of receiving stolen goods, Smith was sentenced to two years' imprisonment.

Upon his release, he stayed a few days with the landlady-"wife", then set off for Leicester to find Caroline — whether in the hope of making things up or with the intention of harming her, one cannot be sure. Either way, it was a choice of evils for Caroline. Luckily for her, she had some loving and brawny brothers, who chased "Mr Love" out of town. But by now Caroline was a bundle of nerves. Deciding that she needed to get far away as fast as possible, she boarded a ship to Canada.

Thirteen years passed before she was summoned back to England to identify as her legal husband the man who had illegally married a number of other women, latterly for the purpose of acquiring a quick profit from a self-imposed state of widowerhood. Caroline was unfortunate in being George Joseph Smith's first, and only real, wife — but she could console herself with the thought that at least the marriage had lasted.

I am not making an original observation, but am merely passing on a remark made by others, when I say that, exceptional to the law of averages, a number of mass-murderers have ostensibly earned their living from trade in secondhand goods.

Of course, this raises an egg-and-hen question: Which came first? Did the need for used items, as stock or to satisfy the stated requirements of customers, cause the dealers to turn to crime — or did these men, criminals first, drift into the trade, perhaps seeing it as a means of reducing their reliance on "fences" for the disposal of loot? Sadly for criminologists who like neat, cut-and-dried findings (and who have been known to fashion them by ignoring details that don't conform), some dealers become criminals . . . and some criminals become dealers.

George Joseph Smith took the latter course. It seems that he started dealing, travelling the country in search of both second-hand wares to buy (or, better, pilfer) and people to buy them, soon after his release from prison in October 1902.

As a profitable sideline to the trade in used goods, he preyed on unused women — virginal spinsters who, with a little flattery, a few promises, a taste of what they had been missing, could be induced to part with a dowry that would lift them off the shelf. As soon as the fleecing was accomplished, Smith made himself scarce. He enjoyed this work, finding in it a mixture of business and pleasure — the pleasure being two-fold, derived partly from the satisfaction to his ego of a play-acting job well done, and partly from what was then referred to as "gratification of strong animal propensities".

Not all of his victims were spinsters. To amend a line of a then-popular song: Oh, he did like to be beside the seaside. Many of his exploits occurred in coastal resorts. In June 1908, when he was in Brighton (one of the towns on the south coast where, nine years before, he had forced his wife Caroline to filch), he struck up a conversation with a widow whom he "just happened to encounter" on the promenade. Mrs F. W. (her name was never revealed) told Smith that she was in Brighton only for the day; that she lived and worked at Worthing, a few miles along the coast. Unfortunately for Mrs F. W., she also gave Smith her address.

The very next day, she received a "gentleman caller". Yes, it was Smith — who, unusually, was using his real name. While Mrs F. W. was still recovering from the shock of seeing him again, he shocked her still more — most pleasurably — by blurting out his belief that the meeting on the front at Brighton had been engineered by Kismet, with some assistance from Cupid, and that, if she did not find him utterly repulsive, she must accept Destiny's word for the fact that she should become his nearest and dearest. Delightedly flabbergasted, the widow murmured something about the need for a period of courtship. But — ever so politely — Smith noted the silver threads among the gold of her hair, said that they ought not to waste a single precious moment, and, his masterfulness making Mrs F. W. reach for the sal volatile, enquired if she had made any engagements for a date three weeks hence that were more pressing than the registry-office wedding he had in mind.

Oh my, such a rush of words. Such a rush that Mrs F. W. treated Smith's question about her worldly goods as an unimportant aside. Having agreed to plight her troth, she introduced George (yes, they were on first-name terms by now) to her best friend — who took an instant and violent dislike to him. Ascribing the friend's reaction to sour grapes, Mrs F. W. travelled with Smith to London. Such a kind man, he insisted on carrying all her baggage; far from complaining of the weight, he fretted that she might have left something of value behind.

In London, they shared an apartment (maybe very properly, maybe with some pre-marital hanky-panky by Smith — Mrs F. W. did not subsequently divulge the sleeping arrangements). The widow was taken on two outings in the metropolis: first, to the north of the city, where Smith insisted on showing her round an interesting new post office — and, while they were there, persuaded her to withdraw her savings . . . and to give the cash to him for safe keeping. Second, to the western outskirts, where Smith treated her to an evening of greyhound racing — and after telling her that he would only be gone a minute, dashed back to the apartment. By the time she got there, not only was there no sign of Smith but there was an entire absence of her belongings.

With money realized from these, together with the widow's savings, Smith opened a secondhand furniture shop in Bristol. In a house just a few doors along the road, a young woman named Edith Pegler lived with her mother. Learning that she was seeking a job, Smith asked her to be his housekeeper. Edith soon discovered that her new employer could not afford to pay her wages; but even sooner than that, she was under his spell.

They were married — Smith for the umpteenth bigamous time — on 30 July 1908. I give the exact date only to illustrate the speed of Smith's romantic conquests, the brevity of the period between his first meeting with a woman and, if he felt that the journey to a registry office was really necessary, the wedding ceremony: Mrs F. W.'s withdrawal of her savings from the North London post office was effected on 3 July, less than four weeks before Edith Pegler became — or *thought* she had become — Mrs Smith.

"Mrs Smith" is correct: at the Bristol registry office, Smith was for the first time "married" under his real name — perhaps because, for once in his life, he felt a slight affection towards a woman. Edith was less cruelly treated than were the rest of his dupes. Aside from the fact that Smith actually provided her with a trousseau (he didn't let on to Edith that it had come from the "bottom drawer" of a young skivvy he had fleeced in the seaside town of Bournemouth), he never, not once, used her as a criminal accomplice; so far as she knew, when for long stretches he was away from home, he was "about the country dealing". In the year following the wedding, while doing some deals in Southampton — another coastal town, notice — he met and went through a form of marriage with a girl who was quite nicely-off. After a honeymoon of a few hours, he left her penniless.

His next port of call was the Essex seaside town of Southend, where he invested most of the Southampton girl's money in a house. The transaction completed, he returned to Bristol.

One day during the summer of 1910, while he was sauntering in Clifton, on the western outskirts of Bristol, his predatory gaze fell upon a girl named Bessie Mundy.

She was destined to be his first murder-victim.

A slim, plain-featured spinster, Bessie Mundy was thirty-three: five years younger than the man with the icicle-blue eyes who introduced himself as Henry Williams when she was out walking near her home in Clifton. Her father, a bank manager, had died a year or so before, leaving her well provided for; she had £2,500 in gilt-edged securities — the equivalent of some £70,000 today.

That made her irresistibly attractive to Smith. He wooed her, won her, and wedded her (or so she thought; she was not to know that the ceremony at Weymouth registry office did not legitimize the relationship, for the simple reason that Smith, not yet a widower, never divorced, had gone through the same ceremony any number of times before).

On the very wedding day, 26 August 1910, Smith wrote to Bessie's solicitor, requesting a copy of her late father's will. When this turned up, Smith may have said a few rude words, because the document showed that the bequest to Bessie was protected; she received an income of a mere £8 a month. Still, he was slightly cheered to learn that the solicitor held £130-odd to cover emergencies. So far as Smith was concerned, an emergency had just arisen: he inveigled the liquid funds from the solicitor.

Not content with these, he rifled Bessie's handbag before absconding. The next morning, she received a letter — bearing no address, of course — that began:

> Dearest, I fear you have blighted all my bright hopes of a happy future. I have caught from you a disease which is called the bad disorder. For you to be in such a state proves you could not have

George Joseph Smith

Bessie Mundy

Alice Burnham

Margaret Lofty

kept yourself morally clean. . . . Now for the sake of my health and honour and yours too I must go to London and act entirely under the doctor's advice to get properly cured of the disease. . . .

In fact, Smith took a train to Bristol, not London, and there rejoined Edith Pegler. He did not stay in Bristol long, but, with the faithful Edith in tow, went on a circular tour, wheeling and dealing as he travelled, returning to Bristol towards the end of 1911.

After seven weeks — reasonably happy ones for Edith, despite Smith's frugality with housekeeping money — his wanderlust took him away again. Though Edith was left virtually penniless, she somehow managed to survive on her own for five months; then she returned to her mother.

In March 1912, Smith's travels took him to the Somerset coastal resort of Weston-super-Mare. By a dreadful coincidence, Bessie Mundy was staying at a boarding-house in the town. One morning, she went out to buy some flowers as a gift for the landlady, Mrs Sarah Tuckett, who was also a family friend. As she walked along the front, she saw Smith (or Henry Williams, as she knew him) staring at the sea.

Certain criminologists subscribe to the theory of "victimology" — a belief that, in many cases, particularly of murder, the victim is more or less responsible for his or her own plight. I can think of no person who more blatantly supports the theory than Bessie Mundy. Considering how Smith had deceived her, robbed her, divested her of self-esteem, and, adding acid to the lemon, accused her of infecting him with a venereal disease, one would suppose that she had but two choices when she saw him — to rush back to the sanctuary of the boarding house or to report her sighting to the police.

But no; she did neither of those things. Incredibly, what she did was to approach Smith, timidly cough to announce her presence, and, once he had recognized her, ask how he was keeping. The moth, wings seared by fire, had returned to the flame.

Mrs Tuckett received a bunch of daffodils — not from her

excited guest but from Bessie's "long-lost husband". The flowers did not help to dispel the landlady's dislike or suspicion of Smith. When he said that he had been scouring the country for his dear Bessie for over a year, Mrs Tuckett enquired why he had not got in touch with her relatives, whose addresses he knew, or with her solicitor. There was no answer to that. Mrs Tuckett told Smith that she intended to send a wire to one of Bessie's aunts. He left Weston-super-Mare that night. And Bessie, who earlier had informed the landlady that she had "forgiven the past", went with him.

The reunited couple travelled around, staying in lodgings, until late in May 1912, when they turned up at Herne Bay, Kent, and rented a house, No. 80 in the High Street, for thirty shillings a month.

They had been in the town for only a few days when Smith consulted a local solicitor about Bessie's "protected" £2,500. Was the protection absolute? What if Bessie were to make a will in his favour? Would all her money be his if she died?

The solicitor received counsel's opinion on 2 July.

It was Bessie Mundy's death warrant.

Less than a week later, she and Smith made mutual wills.

Next day, Smith went into an ironmonger's shop, and after some haggling, agreed to buy a £2 bath for £1.17s.6d. Though he didn't pay for the bath on the spot, the ironmonger agreed to deliver it that afternoon.

Smith's purchase would have surprised Edith Pegler, for in all the time she had lived with him, he had only taken a bath once, perhaps twice. And he had advised her, "I would not have much to do with baths if I were you, as they are dangerous things. It has often been known for women to lose their lives in them, through having fits and weak hearts."

One wonders how Bessie viewed the acquisition. Perhaps, poor creature, she thought back to the letter that had accused her of transmitting a venereal disease, in which a line following those I have quoted said that she had either "had connections with another man . . . or not kept [herself] clean". Maybe she inferred that Smith, concerned at the insufficiency of her personal hygiene but no longer wishing to offend her, had bought the bath as a tacit hint. Did she vow to herself that she would plunge into the bath morning, noon and night, scouring her meagre body of all perhaps contagious impurities?

There is no way of answering such questions. Bessie herself was the only person who could have said what went through her mind. But she was alone, friendless, far from anyone in whom she might confide; Smith had seen to that. In any case, she had precious little time left in which to speak of matters involving her husband; to speak of anything.

After the arrival of the bath, Smith was as busy as a bee in creating the impression that he feared for the life of his beloved Bessie.

The ironmonger delivered the bath during the afternoon of Tuesday, 9 July. Next morning, Smith took Bessie to see Dr Frank French — who, as it happened, was the least-experienced medical practitioner in the town. Smith said that his wife had had a fit. The young doctor may have wondered whether Bessie was suffering from amnesia as well as epilepsy, for she did not remember having a fit. French prescribed a general sedative.

Two days later, Smith called the doctor to the house. Bessie was in bed — unnecessarily, it seemed to French, who could see nothing wrong with her. Still, just to be on the safe side, he went back to the house later in the day. Bessie looked "in perfect health". And she felt fine, she told the doctor — just a touch of tiredness, but that was probably because of the heat-wave.

The touch of tiredness must have evaporated soon after the doctor's departure, for she then wrote a letter to an uncle in the West Country. The letter, which went off by registered post that evening, spoke of *two* "bad fits", and continued:

My husband has been extremely kind and done all he could for me. He has provided me with the attention of the best medical men. . . . I do not like to worry you with this, but my husband has strictly advised me to let all my relatives know and tell them of my breakdown. I have made out my will and have left all I have to my husband. That is only natural, as I love my husband.

At eight o'clock next morning — Saturday, 13 July — Dr French received a note: "Can you come at once? I am afraid my wife is dead."

As soon as the doctor arrived at the house, Smith ushered him upstairs. Bessie was lying on her back in the bath, her head beneath the soapy water. Her face was congested with blood. French lifted the body from the bath and, simply because he thought it might be expected of him, went through the motions of applying artificial respiration, with Smith assisting by holding the dead woman's tongue.

An hour or so later, a coroner's officer took a statement from Smith, and in the afternoon a neighbour, Ellen Millgate, came to the house to lay out the body. Though she was practised at the task, this was the first time that she had found a corpse lying naked and uncovered on bare boards behind a door. Odd, she thought.

Just as odd, when one comes to think of it, was the fact that the doctor had found the body still submerged, the face staring up as if through a glass darkly. Surely the natural thing for Smith to have done when he first entered the room was to lift his wife, or at least raise her head, from the water.

But neither of these oddities, nor any of the several others, perplexed the coroner or his jury, whose verdict was relayed to Bessie's relatives in a note written by Smith on the Monday, soon after the proceedings: "The result of the inquest was misadventure by a fit in the bath. The burial takes place tomorrow at 2 p.m. I am naturally too sad to write more today." Until they received this note, the relatives were not even aware that an inquest had been held. And there was no time for them to travel from Bristol to Herne Bay to attend the funeral (which Smith arranged "to be moderately carried out at an expense of seven guineas", the body being interred in a common grave).

Within forty-eight hours of the funeral, Smith sold most of the furniture in the house, returned the bath (which he had not

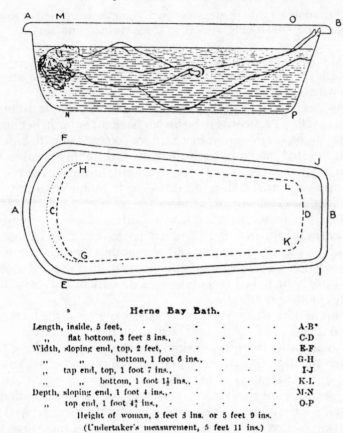

Herne Bay Bath.

Length, inside, 5 feet,	·	·	·	·	A-B*
,, flat bottom, 3 feet 3 ins.,		·	·	·	C-D
Width, sloping end, top, 2 feet,	·	·	·	·	E-F
,, ,, bottom, 1 foot 6 ins.,		·	·	·	G-H
,, tap end, top, 1 foot 7 ins.,		·	·	·	I-J
,, ,, bottom, 1 foot 1½ ins.,	·	·	·	·	K-L
Depth, sloping end, 1 foot 4 ins.,	·	·	·	·	M-N
,, top end, 1 foot 4¾ ins.,	·	·	·	·	O-P

Height of woman, 5 feet 3 ins. or 5 feet 9 ins.

(Undertaker's measurement, 5 feet 11 ins.)

paid for) to the ironmonger, and, most important, instructed the solicitor who only nine days before had drawn up Bessie's will to obtain probate.

By the middle of September, Smith was better off by about £2,500. He was then back in Bristol, again living with Edith Pegler. It appears that, no more than a month or so after his return from Herne Bay, Smith came close to letting Edith in on the secret of how he made money from matrimony: he enlisted her aid in arranging insurance on the life of a young governess, but then for some reason decided not to go ahead with whatever scheme he had in mind.

If that scheme had been carried through, requiring him to remain in Bristol, he might never have met Alice Burnham; and she, a twenty-five-year-old nurse, rosy-cheeked and ample-bosomed, would probably have attained the age of twenty-six.

Smith first encountered Alice in Southsea on a late-summer day in 1913. Having quizzed her about her financial situation, he proposed marriage and was delightedly accepted. Whereas he had gone out of his way to avoid meeting relatives of his earlier victims, he insisted on visiting Alice's father, a fruit-grower living at Aston Clinton, Buckinghamshire. His insistence was entirely due to the fact that Charles Burnham was looking after £100 of his daughter's money. The visit, at the end of October, was not a success. Contrary to Alice's starry-eyed, rose-coloured view of her beau, Mr Burnham considered Smith a man of "very evil appearance — a bad man".

But Alice, ignoring her father's fear that "something serious would happen" if she went ahead with the marriage, became "Mrs Smith" (yes, George was using his real name this time) on 4 November. The day before, her life had been insured for £500.

Owing to some irritating hold-ups (to do with the nest-egg Alice had left with her father, the life insurance, and the making of her will), Smith had to wait over a month before he could become a widower again. Choosing Blackpool as the scene of his crime, on Thursday, 10 December, he knocked at the door of 25 Adelaide Street, a guest-house run by Mrs Susannah Marsden, and, while Alice loitered by the luggage, asked the landlady if there was a bath in the house. As the answer was no, Smith enquired whether Mrs Marsden knew of a nearby establishment offering bed, board *and bath*.

On Mrs Marsden's recommendation, the couple took lodgings at 16 Regent's Road, where the landlady was Mrs Margaret Crossley. As soon as they had unpacked their bags, they walked to Dr George Billing's surgery at 121 Church Street. Smith, who did all the talking, explained that his wife had a nasty headache. The doctor gave Alice a pretty thorough examination, found nothing wrong, prescribed tablets for the

75

headache and a powder to clear the bowels, and requested a fee of three shillings and sixpence — which Smith, would you believe, paid at once, without haggling.

It may be that Mrs Crossley was willing to make allowance for the trangressions of out-of-season boarders, for at about eight o'clock the following night, Friday, when she saw water pouring down a wall in her kitchen, she did not rush upstairs to complain about the over-full bath. Five or ten minutes later, however, she was summoned upstairs by Smith, who said that he could not get his wife to speak to him. The reason for Alice's taciturnity was that her head was submerged in soapy water.

In many respects, the events that followed were reproductions of events following Bessie Mundy's abrupt demise. Dr Billing was called; he, in turn, called the coroner's officer; on the Monday, an inquest jury took just half an hour to return a verdict of accidental death. Smith negotiated a cheap funeral, took the first steps towards collecting his bequest and the payment from the insurance society, and left the town.

Just before his departure, he reluctantly gave Mrs Crossley part of what he owed her and handed her a card on which he had written a forwarding address in Southsea. The landlady scribbled on the back of the card: "Wife died in bath. I shall see him again some day."

She was right.

How many women did George Joseph Smith marry? And how many did he murder?

One cannot give a sure answer to either question. Certain of his exploits are well-documented; but it is quite possible that he committed crimes that were never ascribed to him. For one thing, he was such a busy rogue that even if he could have been persuaded to tell the truth, the whole truth, and nothing but the truth, some of his matrimonial misdeeds might have slipped his mind; for another, some of his female dupes who remained extant may have decided that discretion was the better part of valour; and for yet another, when he was at last brought to book, some of his victims, or their relatives or friends, may not have connected him with the man they had

known under an alias other than those listed in press reports —
Love . . . Williams . . . Baker . . . James . . . and so on.

"Charles Oliver James" was the name he was using in the
late summer of 1914, when, all within a fortnight, he met,
"married" and left impoverished a young domestic servant
called Alice Reavil.

A month or so later, he was "John Lloyd". That was the
name he gave when introducing himself to Margaret Lofty, a
thirty-eight-year-old spinster with pouting lips and dark hair
that she arranged in kiss-curls over her negligible forehead.
The daughter of a parson, she eked out a meagre existence as a
companion to elderly women residing in tranquil cathedral-
cities. Sadly appropriate to her fate, it was in Bath that she first
encountered Smith.

As her savings of £19 were ludicrously inadequate to
Smith's purpose in marrying her, he added to his proposal
instructions regarding life insurance. Once the first — and, as
it turned out, only — premium was paid, he married Margaret
at a registry office. The date was 17 December, a Thursday —
almost exactly a year after the death of Alice Burnham; two
and a half years since the death of Bessie Mundy.

That evening, after Smith had been refused lodgings at one
house in North London (because the landlady was frightened
by his "evil appearance"), he took a room for himself and his
bride at 14 Bismarck Road, Highgate, having first ascertained
that there was a bath in the house.

The grim routine began. Before unpacking, Smith took
Margaret to see a Dr Bates, and told him that his wife was
suffering from a bad headache. It seemed to the doctor that she
was terrified to speak. Next morning, the couple visited a
solicitor for the making of Margaret's will, then went to a post
office to withdraw the balance in her savings account.

In the evening, just after eight o'clock, Louisa Blatch, the
landlady, was doing some ironing in her kitchen. She heard "a
sound of splashing — then there was a noise as of someone
putting wet hands or arms on the side of the bath . . . then a
sigh".

His mission accomplished, Smith crept down the stairs. He

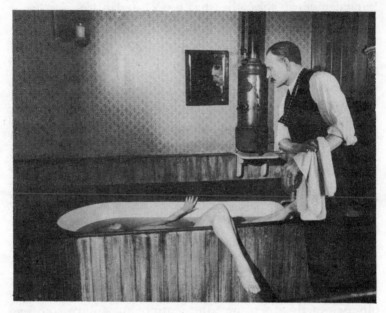

Madame Tussaud's reconstruction of the scene in the bathroom in Bismarck Road. (The bath and geyser came from the scene of the crime.)

entered the parlour, seated himself at the harmonium, and began to play "Nearer My God to Thee".

After the short recital, Smith wandered into the kitchen to ask Mrs Blatch if she had seen anything of his wife. He then went upstairs, "found" Margaret lying dead in the bath, and shouted to the landlady for help.

Subsequent events were almost carbon-copies of those that had followed the drownings in Herne Bay and Blackpool. But there was one important addition: the inquest, with its verdict of accidental death, was reported in the *News of the World* under the double headline,

FOUND DEAD IN BATH
BRIDE'S TRAGIC FATE ON DAY AFTER WEDDING

Though the bereaved husband's name was given as "Lloyd", two readers of the report were so struck by similarities between the tragedy in North London and the death of Alice Smith (*née* Burnham) in Blackpool a year before that they decided to communicate with the police. One of the persons who put two and two together was Joseph Crossley, the husband of the Blackpool landlady; the other was Charles Burnham, the Buckinghamshire fruit-grower whose daughter had drowned in the bath at Mrs Crossley's boarding-house.

Detective Inspector Arthur Neil was put in charge of the investigation. In seeking to untangle the web of Smith's deceits over a period of some sixteen years, Neil and his helpers made inquiries in forty towns, took statements from 150 witnesses, and traced some of the proceeds of Smith's crimes to more than twenty bank accounts.

It didn't take the detectives long to find sufficient evidence to justify Smith's arrest — but the fact that, at the time of his arrest, the investigators knew nothing of the death of Bessie Mundy at Herne Bay adds point to Neil's subsequent observation that there would probably never be a full account of the life and crimes of George Joseph Smith.

At his trial, which was held at the Old Bailey in the summer of 1915, the indictment referred only to the case of Bessie Mundy — who, so far as was known, was the first of Smith's "brides" to die a watery death. His fate was sealed when the judge, Mr Justice Scrutton, allowed the prosecution to introduce evidence relating to the deaths of Alice Burnham and Margaret Lofty, so as to prove his "system" of murder.

Smith was an unruly defendant. He flung abuse at witnesses (describing Mrs Crossley as a lunatic, Inspector Neil as a scoundrel), and when one of his counsel advised him to be quiet, pounded the rail of the dock with his fist and shouted, "I don't care what you say!"

He was silent, however, while Bernard Spilsbury, the pathologist, was giving evidence. Before the trial, in seeking answers concerning the method used for the three murders, Spilsbury had enlisted a nurse as a human guinea-pig — with near-fatal effect, for when he had suddenly lifted the nurse's legs so that her head was immersed in bath-water, she had instantly lost consciousness. This experience had convinced Spilsbury that Smith's trio of victims had died from shock rather than drowning.

Smith had a good laugh when a postcard he had sent to Alice Burnham's father in November 1913 was read out:

> Sir, In answer to your application regarding my parentage, etc. My mother was a Buss horse, my father a Cab driver, my sister a rough rider over the arctic regions — my brothers were all gallant sailors on a steam-roller. This is the only information I can give to those who are not entitled to ask such questions.... Your despised Son-in-law, G. Smith.

He did not exercise his right to give evidence on his own behalf — but that does not mean that he remained silent after the case for the Crown had been presented. He muttered and moaned during the closing speeches, and often interrupted the judge's summing-up, claiming at one point, "I am not a murderer — though I may be a bit peculiar."

The jury were out for only twenty minutes. After stating that he thoroughly agreed with the verdict of Guilty, the judge told Smith that he would spare him the usual exhortation to repent: it would be a waste of time.

The sentence of death was carried out on 13 August, a Friday. Before he was launched into eternity, Smith asserted, with evident conviction, "I shall soon be in the presence of God" — a prophecy that, for God's sake, one trusts was over-optimistic.

The Secret of Ireland's Eye;
A Detective Story

William Roughead

O, that it were possible we might
But hold some two dayes conference with the dead!
From them I should learne somewhat, I am sure,
I never shall know here.

Dutchesse of Malfy.

"People who like legal mysteries and the arts of the literary detective" — the phrase is Andrew Lang's — can hardly fail to appreciate the Kirwan case.[1] It presents a puzzle sufficiently perplexing to intrigue even a blasé taste, and to stimulate the Sherlockian spirit that sleeps in the bosom of the most blameless of Watsons. It is, in the first place, a trial for murder quite out of the common run. The circumstances of the crime, if crime in fact there was, were at the time unprecedented: the drowning of a wife by her husband; and they remained unparalleled in our annals until the revelations made upon a trial in 1915, when one Mr Smith was found to have eclipsed the achievement of his forerunner of the 'fifties by drowning no less than three wives in succession. But the quantitative element apart, the earlier case is much the more interesting and instructive. Smith was a mere mechanic, ingenious, if you will, and clever at his job; a capable craftsman enough, but lacking imagination and the sense of style. Instead of making his first success a stepping-stone to higher things, he was so stupid as to stereotype his method. Further, none but his counsel, *ex officio*, was ever known to doubt his guilt, whereas many have

---

[1] *Report of the Trial of William Burke Kirwan, for the Murder of Maria Louisa Kirwan, his wife, at the Island of Ireland's Eye, in the County of Dublin, on the 6th September 1852.* By John Simpson Armstrong, Barrister-at-Law. Dublin: Printed by Alexander Thom, 87 Abbey Street, for Her Majesty's Stationery Office. 1853.

maintained the innocence of his predecessor. The staging, too, of the respective tragedies differed markedly in scenic effectiveness. Smith's theatre was the domestic bathroom of drab lodgings in mean streets; Kirwan's a desolate island of the sea. As to motive, Smith was but a footpad, murdering for money; Kirwan's act, if he indeed committed it, was of the passionate cast so tenderly regarded by the law courts of France.

The astute reader will notice that I have safeguarded myself from pronouncing upon Mr Kirwan's guilt. It was an Irish case, vehemently discussed; and although the passage of years ought to have cooled the ashes of that old controversy, I am not going to take any risks. Convicted by a Dublin jury, with the approval of two eminent judges of the Irish bench, the prisoner after a three days' trial was duly sentenced to death. The tide of public opinion, which had set strongly against the accused man from the start, then turned in his favour, and as the result of much popular agitation the question was begged in the usual British fashion — how we love a compromise! — the extreme penalty was remitted, and the convict was sent to Spike Island for life. All of which pleased nobody and left the subject in dispute precisely where it was before.

Personally, in the matter of alleged judicial errors I am rather sceptical. Miscarriages of justice have, of course, from time to time occurred, owing to the fallibility of the human agents, but this danger is now discounted by the opportunity provided for review by a competent tribunal. It may be that a Court of Criminal Appeal, had such been available, might on the merits have reversed the jury's finding. Certainly, it was a narrow case; the evidence was purely circumstantial and called for very nice and cautious estimation; had the trial happened to be held in Scotland, our national *via media* of Not Proven would probably have been followed. In hearing, reading, or writing about these cases I always feel how much there is behind the scenes that one ought to know in order to arrive at a fully informed judgment; how much that, by reason of sundry rules of the game played by counsel with the prisoner's life for stake, is never allowed to come out in court.

Thus in the present instance we know next to nothing of the personality of the man, upon which the solution of the problem so largely depends, or apart from the evidence of a single quarrel are we told anything of his usual relations with his wife. The second "Mrs Kirwan" is not produced, and on the important question as to the lawful wife's knowledge of her rival's claims, or even of her existence, we have no information beyond the opposed statements of the contending counsel. Relatives and family friends could have dispelled these doubts and also have settled the vital matter of the dead lady's general health and habits: the Crown representing her as a perfectly sound, healthy woman; the defence, as an epileptic. Again, she is alleged at once to have been a strong and daring swimmer, and not to have been able to swim a stroke! Upon these and many other points the state of proof is disappointingly nebulous. The medical evidence, too, is unsatisfactory and inconclusive. The conditions were plainly unfavourable, but surely nowadays science should be equal to giving a more decisive answer.[1] What weighs most with me is the conduct of Mr Kirwan himself, in the brief glimpses we get of him on the island and after his return to Howth. And those dreadful screams, heard over the water by the five witnesses, re-echo across the years today in a very ugly and suggestive manner for such as have ears to hear.

A mile off the harbour of Howth, in County Dublin, lies the little island with the picturesque name: Ireland's Eye. Visitors to that agreeable watering-place are in the habit of taking boat to the romantic and rocky isle, lying so invitingly in view out in the sea, for purposes "not unconnected", as the newspapers say, with picnics. A ruined chapel of St Nessan, a Martello tower, a fine stretch of beach, a beautiful and extensive prospect: these form the chief attractions. Upon the seaward side a narrow creek or gully, called the Long Hole, will claim our special attention later. Altogether it is a pleasant spot in which to while away the hours of a summer day, and the last

---

[1] See the conclusions of Dr Devon on the medical aspects of the case, p.113.

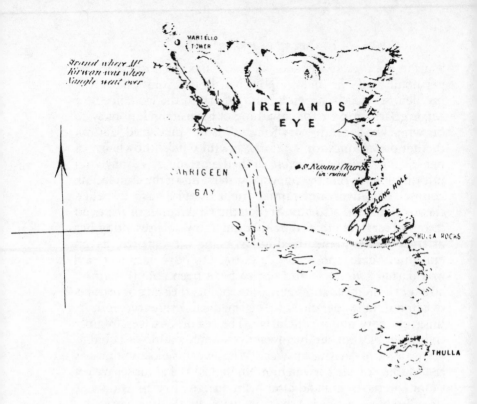

place one would associate with a treacherous and cruel crime.

At 10 a.m. on Monday, 6 September 1852, two persons embarked at the harbour in the boat of a local fisherman named Patrick Nangle. They had with them a bag and a hand-basket, their object being to spend the day upon the island, as they had already done on two or three former occasions. The stout, dark man of about five-and-thirty was Mr William Burke Kirwan, an artist; the handsome, well-made woman of thirty was his wife, Maria Louisa Kirwan; the bag contained the materials of his art, together with the bathing-costume, cap, and bath-sheet of his spouse, a constant and enthusiastic bather; the basket held provisions for an exiguous alfresco meal. Married for twelve years and without a family, the Kirwans lived at No. 11 Upper Merrion Street, Dublin. They were then staying in summer lodgings at Howth, where they had been for some six weeks; and as they

84

were to return to Dublin on the morrow, this was their last excursion.

A commonplace couple enough, one should say; and yet Mr Kirwan's domestic habits present on closer acquaintance certain singular features. Though then on holiday, it was his custom, in his landlady's phrase, to "sleep out" three times a week, going on these occasions to Dublin and returning to Howth next day. Such periodic abstentions from the family bosom were not, as one might suppose, due to the exigencies of his profession as an anatomical draughtsman and furnisher of coloured maps in the city. No; during the whole period of his married life Mr Kirwan had been leading what is figuratively termed a double life. He kept a mistress, one Teresa Kenny, by whom he had no fewer than seven children, and he maintained his Hagar and her brood in a house in Sandymount, a suburb of Dublin, provided her with a servant, and endowed her with the style and title of "Mrs Kirwan". To what extent his legitimate lady was aware of this redundant ménage, and if she knew of it, how she viewed the pluralistic peculiarities of her lord, there is no proof. Upon this point the prosecuting counsel thus addressed the jury:

> It so happened, or was so managed, that neither Maria Kirwan nor Teresa Kenny had either of them the least notion or idea of each other's existence until a comparatively recent period. . . . These facts, gentleman, will appear in the evidence; nay, more, with such consummate art was this system of double deception carried on, that it was only within the last six months that either of these two women became aware of the fact that each had a rival in the prisoner's affections.

Not only did these facts *not* appear in the evidence, but counsel for the defence in his speech declared:

> The connection alluded to was not a new one; his wife knew of it and forgave it, and she and her husband were reconciled.

Here, again, no evidence is produced in support of this statement, and we must choose between the *ipse dixit* of learned counsel on each side of the bar. Whether or not an attractive young wife would be likely to acquiesce to such an arrangement is for the reader to judge, according to his experience of human nature.

Despite the famous dictum of Mr Justice Stephen in the Maybrick case, adultery of itself is not necessarily an incitement to murder. If it were so, I am afraid our criminal courts would be sadly congested. The domestic atmosphere of the Kirwan home, however, is unusually dense, and does need more light than the trial affords. As we shall find, the husband had been heard of late to beat and abuse his wife, and even to threaten her life, acts which exceed the customary amenities of the married state. But more of this later: we are keeping our pleasure-seekers waiting.

They landed below the Martello tower at the north-west corner of the isle, and the boatman was instructed to return for them at eight o'clock — a long day, and a late hour for the autumn season; the sun set that evening at 6.36. At noon Nangle's boat came again to the island, bringing over another family party, who remained there till four o'clock. During the day these people saw the Kirwans, singly and together, at various times and places, but did not speak to them. When leaving in the afternoon for Howth one of the party, observing that the lady looked intently after the boat, called to her, did she wish to go ashore? but she answered, no; the men were to come back for her at eight. So for the next four hours this man and woman remained alone together upon the isle. What passed between them can never be known; no human eye could see how they employed their time, nor watch the act which certainly brought about the violent death of one of them. But human ears, by a strange chance, heard something of that unwitnessed tragedy. The shadows lengthened, the daylight waned, there was a heavy shower about six o'clock, and still silence brooded over the island, wrapped in the gathering dusk.

At seven o'clock a fishing boat, making for Howth harbour, passed Ireland's Eye to the west of the isle, within ten perches of the Martello tower. She was a hooker of 38 tons, with a crew of nine men, of whom one only was then on deck, the steersman, Thomas Larkin. It was "between day and dark". As the boat glided by before a light north-west breeze — the night was quiet and there was no sea — Larkin was startled by a loud scream, "a great screech," from the direction of the Eye. He stood to leeward of the helm and looked towards the island. No one was visible on the shore, though there was light enough in the sky for him to have seen anyone there. In five or six minutes, during which the boat increased her distance, he heard a second scream, but lower; and two minutes afterwards, more faintly, a third. The boat was by then half way to the harbour. The cries were like those of a person in distress; he mentioned the matter at the time to his mates, who being below heard nothing. Night had fallen when they reached Howth.

Four other people on the mainland severally heard these cries. Alicia Abernethy lived at Howth, near the harbour. Her house was directly opposite the Long Hole, a mile off across the water. That evening she called her next-door neighbour to ask the time, and was told it was five minutes past seven. She returned, and while leaning over her garden wall, looking towards the Long Hole on the Eye — "it was between the two lights" and she could just see the island — she heard "a dreadful screech, as of a person in agony and pain". She then heard another, not so loud, and next a weaker one. The cries, she thought, were those of a woman. She told her family about them that night. Catherine Flood, employed in a house on the quay of Howth, was standing at the hall door at five or six minutes past seven, when she heard "great screams" from Ireland's Eye. The first was the loudest — "a very wild scream"; the last was cut off in the middle. There was a minute or two between them. John Barrett, from the door of his house at the east pier, heard about seven o'clock "screeches abreast the harbour". Going over to the pier, he heard two or three more; they declined in loudness and seemed to come from Ireland's Eye. Hugh Campbell, "between day and dark", was leaning over the quay wall, when he heard from the direction of the island three cries, "resembling the calling of a person for assistance"; some three minutes elapsed between the cries, which became successively weaker. *Half an hour later he saw Nangle's boat leave the harbour and go over to the island.*[2] He had often before heard voices from the Eye.

These five persons were all reputable folk of the place, credible witnesses, whose testimony cross-examination failed to shake. So we have the fact clearly proved that about seven o'clock that night there rang out upon that little isle three lamentable screams of terror and distress, so piercing as to be audible a mile off upon the mainland. But Mr Kirwan, rendered deaf by anxiety for, or indifference to the fate of, his vanished wife, or wholly engrossed with his sketch-book in making the most of the failing light, as appears, heard nothing.

At twenty minutes to eight o'clock Patrick Nangle, and his cousin Michael, accompanied by two other men, left Howth harbour as arranged to bring back the pleasure-seekers. The boat reached the island about eight o'clock, and landed close to the tower. It was then getting very dark and they saw nothing of their party; but on their calling out, the voice of Mr Kirwan replied, "Nangle, come up for the bag." Patrick went ashore; he found Mr Kirwan standing by himself on the bank and received from him his bag and sketchbook. Patrick, taking these down to the boat, met Michael going up; who, seeing Mr Kirwan coming towards the boat and finding that he was alone, at once exclaimed, "Where is the mistress?" "I have not seen her for the last hour and a half," was the reply. "Sir," said Michael, "you should have had the mistress here, and not have to be looking for her at this hour of the night; what way did she go?" "She went that way," said Mr Kirwan, pointing in the direction of the Long Hole; "I was sketching at the time. She left me after the last shower. She did not like to bathe where I told her to bathe, because there was a bad smell there." Michael and Mr Kirwan then went to look for her along the strand, Patrick going back to the boat. "Maria, why don't you

[2] This statement is important as disposing of one of the defence theories as to the cries, namely, that they were those of the boatmen and Mr Kirwan, calling for his wife during their search for the missing lady.

answer?" called her husband; "The boat is waiting." Michael too kept calling, "Mrs Kirwan!" but there was no response. Their search included the Long Hole, so far as the state of the tide permitted, and *while there Michael could hear Patrick hailing from beside the tower.*[3] Returning, they found he had been equally unsuccessful. "This is a fine job," said Michael, "to be here at this hour of the night! Where are we to find this woman? Let us leave the other two men in the boat and we will go round again; if Mrs Kirwan comes in the meantime, they can go on the top of the bank and hail us." The three then started to retrace their steps. Descending the rocks into the Long Hole, Mr Kirwan stumbled and fell. At that instant Patrick Nangle cried out that he saw "something white" below.

The Long Hole is an inlet, some 360 feet in length, narrow at the entrance and wider towards the head, enclosed by steep banks and frowned upon by cliffs. From low to high water mark the distance is 163 feet. This area is divided into two channels by a large rock in the middle, 22 feet high, on which the tide rises on the landward side about a foot at high water. The surrounding strand is of coarse gravel, interspersed with lesser rocks, and 12 feet above low-water mark a low barrier of these stretches across the channel, here 28 feet in breadth. Just within this barrier, at the base of the south-eastern side of the gully, is a small rock, 3 feet long and 12 inches high, upon which was found the body of the dead lady.

The tide was out. She lay upon her back, the head hanging down over the edge against the barrier rock, the arms extended, the knees bent, and the feet in a shallow pool. Her wet bathing-dress was gathered up about her arm-pits, leaving the whole body exposed, and beneath her was a wet bathing-sheet, upon which she partly lay. Her bathing-cap was missing — it was found a fortnight later at high-water mark, the strings tied in a tight knot — but she wore bathing-boots; seaweed and gravel were entangled in her hair. The body was still quite warm and flexible. The mouth was frothing; there

---

[3] So cries from one end of the isle were audible at the other.

was blood upon the face, blood upon the breasts, and blood was flowing from the ears and from other parts. Patrick, for decency, adjusted the bathing-dress, straightened the arms and legs, and tied the sheet twice about her at the neck and knees, all before Michael and Mr Kirwan, who had been searching the other side of the cove, came up. "Mr Kirwan said, 'Oh Maria, Maria!' " and told the men to look for her clothes: "We would get them there on the rock" — pointing to the high centre rock before mentioned. Patrick went up and searched as directed, but could find nothing. Mr Kirwan then went up himself, and coming back in a few minutes with a shawl and "something white" in his hand, bade Patrick go up again, which the latter did. This time he at once found the clothes in a place where he had already looked without result: "I had searched the very same place before, and did not find them." The shawl was then wrapped about the head; what the "something white" was we shall see in the sequel. Patrick next proposed that the boat be brought round for the body, so he and Michael left accordingly. Mr Kirwan refused to go, and threw himself upon the corpse. It was now about nine o'clock and it took them an hour to fetch the boat; when they reached the Long Hole they found Mr Kirwan just as they had left him, "lying with his face on the breast of the body". The remains, wrapped in a sail, were carried to the boat by one of the men, who got wet up to the knees during the operation, but none of the others got wet, nor, according to them, did Mr Kirwan, who took no part.

Arrived at Howth, the body of Mrs Kirwan was taken on a dray to her lodgings and laid on the floor of her room. Mrs Campbell, the landlady, was short-sighted and much upset: she did not examine it closely; but she saw that Mr Kirwan's legs were wet, and she helped him to change his stockings. Three other women in the house that night proved that his boots, stockings, drawers and trousers were wet, and that as he sat on a chair by the kitchen fire drying them, water dripped from him on to the floor. These dames — one, Mrs Lacy, was a sick-nurse of forty years' standing — were ordered by him to wash the body. When they pointed out to him that the police would not allow it to be touched until an inquest was held, the bereaved husband made this remarkable retort: "I don't care a damn for the police; the body must be washed!" So washed it accordingly was, and laid out as for burial before it was seen by a medical man. Whatever the propriety and whatever the motive of Mr Kirwan's action, there is no doubt that it resulted in the loss of very valuable evidence. The washing was done by Anne Lacy and Catherine M'Garr, one taking the right, the other the left side, while Mary Robinson held a candle. The account given by these women of the appearances noted by them is of the last importance. There was a large quantity of blood on the sail where the lower part of the body had lain. The body was quite limber.

> The face was covered with blood; the blood came from a cut about the eyes, and on the cheek and forehead; the ears were also loaded with blood, which was still running from the inside of them; I spunged and washed the ears, but the blood continued flowing afterwards for nearly half an hour; I had to put a flannel petticoat to prevent it flowing down.

There was a cut on the right breast, which bled freely, and a discharge of blood, which was not natural, from another part. The right side of the body was black from shoulders to feet. The lips were much swollen, the eyes "as red as blood", the neck slightly twisted. The body was healthy looking and finely formed: "She was a beautiful creature". Thus Mrs Lacy, whose long experience gives weight to her testimony. Mrs M'Garr noticed wounds about the eyes, "as if torn". The nose was "crooked", the lips swelled and covered with slime, blood flowed from the ears, the left breast, and from another part. Mary Robinson observed that the eyes were bloodshot and the ears bleeding. These details, though repellent, are essential to a determination of how this lady came by her death.

Between one and two o'clock on the following day, Tuesday 7 September, by order of the Coroner the body was professionally examined. Of distinguished members of the faculty there was then as now no lack in County Dublin, and it seems unfortunate that the duty was entrusted to a medical student, named Hamilton, who stated his qualifications as "having been attending lectures during the last six years". He made what he himself describes as "a superficial examination", the result of which will presently appear, and having no reason to suspect foul play, he assumed it to be a case of simple drowning and reported accordingly. The inquiry opened later in the afternoon before Mr Coroner Davis, the authorities having apparently no suspicion that the death was other than fortuitous. The Nangle cousins were examined. "Mr Kirwan took an active part in the investigation," said the Coroner at the subsequent trial; "I remember his interrupting one of the witnesses who was giving his testimony; I do not remember what he said to him; I believe the witness in question was one of the Nangles." Now, as appears from the evidence of Patrick Nangle at the trial, just as he was beginning to tell the Coroner about the sheet and the finding of the clothes, he was interrupted by Mr Kirwan and was "put back", another witness being called. Thus as to these most material facts he "was not allowed to speak". The evidence of Mr Kirwan was as follows:—

I am an artist, residing at No 11 Upper Merrion Street, Dublin. The deceased lady, Maria Kirwan, was my wife; I was married to her about nine or ten years. I have been living with Mrs Kirwan in Howth for five or six weeks. I was in the habit of going over to Ireland's Eye as an artist. Mrs Kirwan used to accompany me; she was very fond of bathing, and while I would be sketching she would amuse herself roaming about or bathing. Yesterday we went over as usual. She bathed at the Martello tower on going over, but could not stay long in the water as the boatmen were to bring another party to the island. She left me in the latter part of the day, about six o'clock, to bathe again. She told me she would walk round the hill after bathing and meet me at the boat. I did not see her alive afterwards, and only found the body as described by the sailors.

It will be observed that no mention was made by Mr Kirwan of the three screams, and that he did not allege, as was later done in his behalf, that his wife was subject to epilepsy. The five witnesses who heard the cries had not then come forward. Neither the landlady nor the women who washed the corpse were examined. Upon these insufficient premises the jury founded a verdict of accidental death. Unfortunately for the ends of justice, a grave was chosen in the wettest part of the cemetery at Glasnevin, the remains of Mrs Kirwan were buried there, and the affair seemed in a fair way to be forgotten.

If Mr Kirwan was innocent of his wife's death he was curiously unlucky in his reputation. The fact that he had a mistress with seven children became generally known and raised a strong prejudice against him in the public mind. He was even said to have committed bigamy with her, but the woman, as appears, was merely a chronic concubine. One Mrs Byrne, his next-door neighbour in Dublin, did not scruple to promulgate his guilt. Indeed, this lady had foretold the event: "Kirwan had taken his wife to some strange place to destroy her"; and being but human she was naturally gratified by the fulfilment of her prophecy. She further alleged that "Bloody Billy," as she impolitely termed him, had murdered her own husband.[4] Two other charges of murder were also brought against Mr Kirwan in the Dublin press. It was there stated,

(1) "That in 1837, he, Kirwan, burglariously entered Bowyer's house in Mountjoy Street, and carried away Bowyer's property, which he converted to his own use; and that for this offence he was tried before the Recorder, and only escaped upon a point of law."
(2) "That having thus obtained possession of Bowyer's property, he murdered him."
(3) "That in order to keep Mrs Bowyer quiet, he paid her an annuity of forty pounds a year, blood money."[5]

Whatever be the truth as to these allegations, it is plain that Mrs Bowyer, like Father Paul of the *Bab Ballads*, did such

[4] *The Kirwan Case: illustrating the Danger of Conviction on Circumstantial Evidence.* Dublin: James Bernard Gilpin, 59 Dame Street, 1853.
[5] *Exposure of an Attempt to impute the Murder of Messrs Crowe and Bowyer to William Bourke Kirwan.* Dublin: James Bernard Gilpin, 59 Dame Street, 1853.

things "singularly cheap". The other charge of murder related to his brother-in-law, Mr Crowe. "That Kirwan murdered him, according to the statement of the parties preferring the charges, was beyond all doubt because he accompanied him to Liverpool, and Crowe was not heard of since."[6]

The Nangles and the nurses talked of the amount of blood they had seen about the body, and a report spread that the deceased had been done to death with a sword cane. Then Mrs Kirwan had been a Catholic and her husband was a Protestant, facts which in Ireland are still of more than spiritual import, and belief in Mr Kirwan's guilt or innocence became largely a matter of faith. Finally, the authorities realized that the case was one which called for further investigation, so the body was ordered to be exhumed. On 6 October — thirty-one days after death — Dr George Hatchell, assisted by Dr Tighe, made a post-mortem examination, the results of which will presently appear.[7] The coffin was found to be lying in two and a half feet of water, due to the dampness of the soil. Following upon the doctors' report, Mr Kirwan was apprehended on a charge of murder. The warrant was executed at his own house in Dublin, where the police found Miss Kenny and her young brood installed in the dead wife's room.

The trial, originally fixed for November, was at the instance of the accused postponed, and did not open till Wednesday, 8 December 1852, when it took place before a Commission of Oyer and Terminer held at Green Street, Dublin, the presiding judges being the Hon. Philip C. Crampton and the Right Hon. Richard W. Greene. John George Smyly, QC, Edmund Hayes, QC, and John Pennefather conducted the prosecution; Isaac Butt, QC, Walter Burke, QC, William W. Brereton, QC and John A. Curran appeared for the defence. The charge against the accused was that on 6 September, at Ireland's Eye in the County of Dublin, he "did wilfully, feloniously, and of his

---

[6] *Ibid.*

[7] Counsel for the prisoner at the trial complained that the Crown did not call Dr Tighe; but if that gentleman dissented from the opinion expressed by his colleague, he could have been called for the defence.

malice prepense kill and murder one Maria Louisa Kirwan",
to which he pleaded "Not Guilty". Mr Smyly, in the case for
the Crown, proceeded to call witnesses in support of the
indictment.

The first was Alfred Jones, surveyor, who had prepared
plans of the *locus* and made certain calculations and
measurements at the Long Hole. The place where the clothes
were found was about the middle of the central rock, 5 feet 6
inches above the strand, and at high tide 1 foot 6 inches out of
the water. On 6 September it was high water at 3.30 p.m., and
at that hour there would be 7 feet of water over the "body"
rock; at 6.30, 2 feet 6 inches; at 7, 1 foot 9 inches; at 7.15, 1
foot 4½ inches; at 7.30, 1 foot; at 8, 3 inches; and at 9.30 the
tide would be 2 feet below the "body" rock. The distance from
the Martello tower to the Long Hole was 835 yards; from
where Mr Kirwan was standing when the boat arrived, 792
yards. Cross-examined by Mr Butt, a person about to bathe
might step down to the strand from the rock where the clothes
were found.

Mrs Margaret Campbell told how the Kirwans came to her
as lodgers in June, and of Mr Kirwan's habit of absenting
himself three nights a week. During the first month of their
stay she noticed quarrelling between them more than once.

> I heard angry words from Mr Kirwan to his wife. I heard him
> say, "he would make her stop there"; I heard him miscall her; I
> heard him call her a strumpet. I heard him say, "I'll finish you!" I
> do not think they had been a month with me at that time. On the
> same evening I heard her say to him, "Let me alone, let me alone!"
> Next morning I heard her say to him she was black from the usage
> she had got the preceding night — across her thighs.

Witness heard a rush in their room, and "thought he beat her".
There was no one else in the house at the time except Anne
Hanna, who was with witness in the kitchen. Mrs Kirwan used
to bathe every day at the ladies' bathing-place. She was in good
health all the time she was in Howth. On the Thursday and
Friday before her death she and her husband spent the day on

Ireland's Eye, returning home about nine o'clock. Mrs Campbell then described the bringing back of the body, and the condition of Mr Kirwan's nether garments, as before narrated. Cross-examined by Mr Butt, she had heard them quarrelling at different times; it was on the first occasion that she heard the threatening language; subsequently "they had an odd word now and again"; he never used violence but the once. She had heard Mrs Kirwan's mother, Mrs Crowe, caution her not to be too venturesome in bathing.

Anne Hanna, who washed for Mrs Kirwan, corroborated as regards the first quarrel. She heard the furniture being knocked about, and a man's voice say, "I'll end you, I'll end you!"

Patrick Nangle described the happenings on the island with which we are already acquainted. When he recovered the sail in which the body had been wrapped, he found a great deal of blood on it: "I had to scrub it with a broom". Cross-examined by Mr Brereton, he was sure the body was not stiff when found; none of the limbs was stiff. There were several scratches about the eyes. The mouth was frothing. Blood flowed from the lower part of the body. The scratches could not have been caused by crabs; there were no crabs where the body lay; Mr Kirwan did not say, when he (witness) saw him on the bank, that his wife must be in the boat. There was no swell that night to bruise the body. The injuries could not have occurred by scraping on the gravel. The sheet was under the body when he found it; he saw no shawl until he came back with the boat. He did not care how dark it was: he had searched the rock and found nothing where, after Mr Kirwan had gone up, he found the clothes. He demanded and got £2 for his trouble that night. No one could have been on the island after four o'clock without his knowledge. Mr Kirwan could not have got wet in the pool where the feet lay: there was not enough water in it.

Michael Nangle gave his version of the facts, which, with one exception, tallied with that given by Patrick. He had never before heard of ladies bathing at the Long Hole; the rocks there were sharp and dangerous. He looked for the clothes along the strand; Patrick searched the rock. Mr Kirwan came down "bringing something white in his hand, like a sheet, and also a shawl". Witness did not see the body closely till the next day; he only saw the face, on which were cuts or scratches. Mr Kirwan did not get wet while in their company. The water in the Long Hole was as smooth as in a well. During their search Mr Kirwan seemed "uneasy" — which, in any view, is not surprising.

Michael differed from Patrick only in that he thought the sheet was brought down from the rock by Mr Kirwan, whereas Patrick was positive that the sheet was beneath the body when discovered, *that it was wet,* and that he tied it twice about the body before Michael and Mr Kirwan came up. It was dark at the time; Patrick, who examined and handled the body, is more likely to be right than Michael, who did neither.[8] The significance of the wetness of the sheet, as sworn to by Patrick, appears to have been overlooked: however dark it was, that is a matter on which he could not well be mistaken, and had Mrs Kirwan left the sheet with her clothes upon the rock, it would like them have been dry, for they were found above high-water mark. What, then, was the "something white" selected by Mr Kirwan from his wife's clothes? Most probably, her chemise, which, as we shall find, was missing, while that she wore one will hardly be disputed.

Thomas Giles, one of the boatmen, corrobated the Nangles to the extent of his knowledge, and Arthur Brew, of the picnic party, told what he had seen of the Kirwans when on the island. Then followed the five witnesses who heard the cries. Mr Butt worked hard to bring out minor discrepancies in their statements, such as, for instance, the number of minutes that elapsed between the several screams, and so forth; but upon

---

[8] "Seeing the two men, Patrick and Michael Nangle, and hearing their evidence, we could form no reasonable doubt of the truth of either of them. They are both elderly men. Michael appears older than Patrick, nor is he by any means so observant or so intelligent a man. Patrick Nangle's account of his finding the body with the sheet partly under it, and his tying it across the chest and knees, is perfectly consistent with all the circumstances" — Letter from the Foreman on behalf of himself and ten of the Jury, in *Saunders' News Letter*, 13 January 1853.

the cardinal points that each *did* hear about seven o'clock three distinct screams, decreasing in volume, coming from Ireland's eye, their testimony was unscathed.

The next group of witnesses was the women who had washed and laid out the corpse, and who now deposed to the condition in which they found it, as before described. They stuck gallantly to their guns, and Mr Butt failed to impair the value of their evidence. Mrs Lacy, the dame of forty years' practical experience, maintained in cross-examination: "There was nothing like the bite of a crab on the body." The hearing was adjourned.

Next day, 9 December, began with the evidence of Joseph Sherwood, Sergeant of Constabulary, stationed at Howth. He had seen the face of the body on the night of Mrs Kirwan's death: it was scratched, there was a cut on the right temple, the mouth was swollen, and the eyes were bloodshot. He noticed that Mr Kirwan's clothes were wet from the knees downward. Upon the arrest of that gentleman at his house in Upper Merrion Street, on 7 October, witness there saw the woman Kenny with her children. He was present when the bathing-cap was found at high-water mark in the Long Hole on 11 September; the string was tied in a hard knot. Shouts at Ireland's Eye were audible at Howth; he himself had heard such on the mainland. Cross-examined by Mr Butt, the bundle of Mrs Kirwan's clothes did not include a chemise. The clothes were clean and free from bloodstains.

Ann Molloy, the Kirwan's servant, said she had been with them for twelve months. They had no family. Miss Teresa Kenny was then called, but failed to appear. It would have been interesting to have heard her evidence. William Bridgeford stated that he was the owner of the house in Sandymount occupied by Mr Kirwan, who became his tenant in 1848. Witness saw there occasionally a woman whom he understood to be Mr Kirwan's wife. There were children in the house. He had received notes, presumably on business, from the woman, signed "Teresa". Catherine Byrne, Mr Kirwan's servant at his "home from home", said that a woman lived with him there who was known as "Mrs Kirwan". They had seven children. A strange lady called once to make some inquiries.[9]

Thomas Alexander Hamilton, the medical student who had seen the body, was next examined. It was, he said, then prepared for burial. He made a superficial examination of the head, but found no fracture. There was a scratch on the right temple, and scratches around the eyes, which were closed; he did not open them; the eyelids were livid. The lobe of one of the ears was cut. There was froth, thin, light, and stationary, upon the mouth. The abdomen was full and firm. He did not examine the body very closely, and saw no blood, or anything else that attracted his attention. Cross-examined, he noticed no marks of violence. He had never before examined the body of a drowned person. He knew nothing at the time to excite suspicion.

Dr George Hatchell, who made the post-mortem examination thirty-one days after death, was next called. He was present at the exhumation. The coffin lay in two and a half feet of water, which had entered it, and the body was to a certain extent macerated. The scalp showed no marks of violence. He found abrasions or scratches about the right eye. The eyes were injected with blood. The lobe of the right ear was wanting. There were no other injuries about the ears that he could observe, decomposition being too far advanced. The lips were swollen and very vascular; the tongue was marked above and below by the teeth. On opening the head, the brain was found to be in a semi-fluid state and of a light-pinkish colour. The base of the skull was not fractured. There was nothing remarkable about the trachea and larynx, and the vertebrae of the neck were not dislocated. On the right breast was a superficial cut or scratch. There was extensive lividity on the right side due probably to gravitation of the blood. The lower orifices of the body were swollen and their interior very vascular, much more than was usual. The lungs were

---

[9] One would like to have known the date of this visit and the nature of the inquiries, if, as appears, the caller was the real Mrs Kirwan; but the matter was not carried further.

congested by engorgement of blood; the heart was empty on both sides. He had visited and inspected the *locus*.

> From the appearances you observed on the body, are you able, as a medical man, to form an opinion as to the cause of death, and what is that opinion? — I am of opinion that death was caused by asphyxia, or a sudden stopping of respiration. From the congestion in the . . ., from the engorgement of the lungs, and other circumstances, I should say that in all probability the simple stoppage of respiration must have been combined with pressure of some kind, or constriction, which caused the sudden stoppage. I do not think that simple drowning would produce to the same extent the appearances I saw.

Cross-examined by Mr Butt, the extreme congestion which he had found could not be produced by drowning alone. He had never seen such engorgement caused by simple drowning. There must have been a struggle for life, whether by herself or with another. There was no internal injury to the ears nor any sign of a sharp instrument having been thrust into the body. Bathing on a full stomach might bring on a fit; but he had never heard of a person who fell in a fit of epilepsy giving more than one scream.

Henry Davis, the Coroner who held the inquest on Mrs Kirwan, stated what took place at that investigation. Cross-examined, he said that in his opinion the scratches on the body were due to the bites of green crabs. In re-examination, he described Mr Kirwan's behaviour at the inquiry, as already mentioned.

The case for the Crown closed with the reading of Mr Kirwan's deposition before the Coroner, and Mr Butt addressed the jury for the defence. He began by begging them to dismiss from their minds anything they might have heard out of doors to the prejudice of the accused. The evidence upon which the Crown asked them to conclude that his wife had died by his hands was (first) the appearances of the body, (second) the suspicion against him and the cries from the island, and (third) the stain upon his character as a husband. It was impossible for the prisoner to bring any evidence as to what had happened. He was not a competent witness, and he and his wife were alone upon the island when she met her death. That the cries heard were hers was merely a conjecture; even if they were so, that was consistent with her death in a fit. He asked the jury to disbelieve the evidence of the witnesses who said they heard the cries on the mainland; Larkin's was the only evidence on which they could rely, but the guilt of the prisoner could not be deduced from it. The cries he heard might have been those of Mr Kirwan, calling for his wife before the boat arrived. If this was murder, how did he do it? Did he strangle her? Did he go into the water and drown her? If her death was the result of violence and Larkin heard her death cries, how was it that eight minutes elapsed between the first and the second? What was a strong woman doing in the meantime? It was a natural supposition that she had been attacked by epilepsy on going into the water with a full stomach after her dinner,[10] and that she shrieked first, revived afterwards, and shrieked again. With regard to the prisoner's unfortunate connection, that could supply no motive for the crime. It was an old affair; his wife knew of it and forgave him, and it would be monstrous to suppose that because he had been unfaithful to her he was capable of imbruing his hands in her blood. As to the appearances presented by the body, no marks of violence were found; there was no internal injury to the ears or other parts, and drowning in a fit would account for the bleedings and congestion. Dr Hatchell in his report mentioned "strangulation", but the neck and throat were uninjured. Did he mean by "compression" that she was seized and crushed to death? No force was possible without injuring some vital organ. The cuts and scratches, the Coroner told them, were due to the bites of crabs; or they might have been caused by struggling among the rocks: her hair was full of sand and seaweed. A murderer would not begin by scratching her face, and there were no scratches on *his* face as might have been expected. If he had followed her into the sea and drowned her, his arms and coat would have been wet. He might have got his

---

[10] "The stomach was contracted and empty," *Post-mortem Report.*

feet wet in the very pool in which her feet lay. "If he loved his wife, as it seemed evident that he did," he who flung himself upon the body, and remained so long alone with it, could not be the murderer.[11] As to the position of the sheet and the finding of the clothes, these rested solely on the evidence of Patrick Nangle, to which no weight should be attached; that of Michael Nangle was upon these points preferred. This accusation would never have been brought but for the prisoner's previous character; if they dismissed from their minds that consideration, they should acquit him, and he would leave the court a wiser and a better man.[12]

Two witnesses only were called for the defence, Drs Rynd and Adams, who were present in Court and had heard the evidence. Dr Rynd said the appearances described pointed to death by asphyxia, or stoppage of the breath and circulation. If caused by external violence there should be manifest marks thereof; there were no such injuries here. All the appearances could be produced by a fit of epilepsy, without any concurring cause. An epileptic might give several screams. Bathing with a full stomach would be apt to cause a fit.[13] Congestion of the brain would account for the bleeding from the ears; general congestion for that from other organs. Cross-examined by Mr Smyly, witness admitted he never knew of such bleeding in a case of simple drowning. The blood continued fluid in drowned bodies for a considerable time after death. The amount of congestion would depend on the efforts made by the drowning person to save himself. Counsel referred witness to the notorious case of Burke and Hare, where, although no external marks of violence were visible, suffocation was

---

[11] The case of Dr Pritchard in 1865 affords a sufficient answer to this argument. During the four months in which he was torturing his wife to death, the Doctor habitually slept with her, and she died in his arms. At the funeral, he caused the coffin to be opened that he might kiss her for the last time.

[12] It is noteworthy that Mr Butt omitted to deal with the evidence of Mrs Campbell and of Anne Hanna regarding Mr Kirwan's ill treatment of his wife and his threats against her life. The "don't-care-a-damn-for-the-police" remark at the washing of her body, counsel attributed to a tender solicitude for the remains, rather than the desire to suppress evidence.

[13] Cf. note p. 101.

effected;[14] and asked whether a wet sheet held over the mouth would produce the appearances described, without leaving any marks of violence, Dr Rynd admitted that it would do so. He had seen Mrs Kirwan professionally six years before; she appeared to him a fine strong young woman. He had heard, from a person deeply interested in the trial, that her father had died of epilepsy.[15]

Dr Adams concurred generally in the evidence of Dr Rynd, but admitted that it was unusual for an epileptic to scream more than once — "the first scream is the rule". Cross-examined, a wet cloth over the mouth and nose would produce all the effects of drowning. If a person was half under water it would cause congestion; the longer the struggle, the greater the congestion. It all depended upon the mouth and nose being under water. He had never known a case of accidental drowning where similar bleeding from the organs occurred, nor had he ever heard of a case of epilepsy accompanied by such bleedings. Re-examined, pressure applied to the chest would leave some external marks of violence.[16]

> *Mr Justice Crampton* — Supposing death to have taken place by forcible submersion, or from accidental drowning, would you be able, from the appearances described, to state to which species of death they were attributable? — My Lord, in my opinion, no man living could do so.

The case for the defence being here closed, Mr Hayes replied on the part of the Crown. He told the jury to disregard the rumours which had been circulated to the prisoner's prejudice, and defended the prosecution from the animadversions of Mr Butt. Having reviewed the accused's connection with the woman Kenny, whom he had represented as "Mrs Kirwan", counsel dealt with the quarrel and the threats against his wife's life.

[14] *Burke and Hare.* Edited by William Roughead. Notable British Trials Series. 1921.
[15] This is about as competent evidence as that of "what the soldier said", which Mr Justice Stareleigh disallowed in the leading case of *Bardell v. Pickwick*.
[16] The witness was plainly unacquainted with the evidence in Burke's case, where the contrary was established beyond dispute.

Is it reasonable to suppose that a man who had been living with a concubine for ten years, and during all that time gave her his name, while he was beating his legitimate wife at Howth, could entertain connubial affection for the woman he treated so grossly?

He then described the fatal excursion to the island on 6 September. As to the fact of the three screams, sworn to by five witnesses, there could be no possibility of doubt; that they were the shrieks of epilepsy was an ingenious suggestion, unsupported by proof.

If there was any evidence that this lady had been previously affected by epilepsy or anything of that kind, there might have been a shadow of ground upon which to found the assertion. As the prisoner has forborne to produce such testimony, it is not too much to infer that there was none to produce; we must take it as proved that the deceased was a perfectly healthy woman.

Why did Mr Kirwan say nothing about the screams? He must have heard them; he hadn't seen his wife for an hour; "and yet this affectionate husband is deaf to these dreadful shrieks". If he knew she were subject to fits he would have run to her assistance, but he is found calmly waiting for the boat, and all he says is, "Nangle, come up for the bag"! The first mention of the missing lady comes from the boatman, not from the distracted, agonized husband. Two hours after this lady set out to bathe, the search for her is begun in the dark. At first it is fruitless. They would note that Patrick, calling out near the boat, is heard by Michael at the Long Hole: was it too much to suppose that if the prisoner had been at that part of the island he would hear screams from the Long Hole? The search was renewed, the body was found, and the question now arose, whether, upon all the facts and circumstances of the case, death was caused by accident or by Mr Kirwan. No direct evidence was possible; and it was from circumstantial evidence alone that the jury could arrive at a conclusion. How came that sheet beneath the body? It should have been high and dry for her use when she came out. The position of the bathing-dress, too, was inexplicable. At seven o'clock, if this lady was then bathing, the tide was going out, and there was 1 foot 9 inches of water over the "body" rock, which was a foot high. She was an expert swimmer: was it likely that she should be accidentally drowned there?

Let us suppose her in this water, 2 feet 9 inches deep; let us suppose the prisoner coming into the Hole with the sheet in his hand, after taking it from the place in which it was left, ready to put it over her head; let us suppose she saw his dreadful purpose: can you not then conceive and account for the dreadful shrieks that were heard, when the horrid reality burst upon her mind that on that desolate, lonely island, without a living soul but themselves upon it, he was coming into that Long Hole to perpetrate his dreadful offence? Would not the consequence have been the dreadful shrieks that were heard and sworn to? If he succeeded in putting her under the water, notwithstanding her vain efforts to rise, struggling with all her energy against his greater strength, can you not imagine the fearful, agonizing, and fainter shrieks that men and women from the mainland depose to having heard? That is not mere imagination; it is a rational deduction from the evidence; and it is for you to say whether, upon all the facts of the case, that might not have occurred, or whether the prisoner lost his wife without any fault of his own.

As to what happened when the body was found, Patrick Nangle was a better witness than Michael, who on his own showing saw but little of it. If the deceased left her husband about six o'clock, and if he did not see her thereafter, it was very strange that he should be able at once to know where her clothes lay, in a spot to which he pointed and in which Patrick, who was familiar with the place, had failed to find them. The discrepancy between the Nangles with respect to the sheet was reconciled if what Kirwan brought down from the rock in his hand with the shawl was the chemise. That chemise was not forthcoming: it was for the jury to say whether it was not the "something white" to which Michael referred. With regard to the prisoner's insistence on the washing of the body, he, a gentleman of position and education, was sworn to have said, "I don't care a damn for the police; the body must be washed," although he knew his wife had met her death suddenly on a lonely island, and that every circumstance as to the state of the body was most important to the ends of justice. Moreover, he was actually warned of the coming investigation. The women who washed the body were positive that the scratches were not caused by crabs.

> You will ask yourselves, gentlemen, whether or not these scratches have any reference to the time when the horrible sheet was being put over the face of the deceased; whether at that awful moment she might not have put up her hands to try and remove the sheet, and endeavouring to do so, tore herself in the manner described.

The bathing-cap, found at high-water mark, with the strings tied tight, was also against the supposition of death by epilepsy or accident. Might it not have been torn off in the struggle that took place before the sheet was thrown over her head? Dr Adams, with all his great experience, never knew a case of death from simple drowning or epilepsy in which such bleeding occurred, and yet in the face of that testimony they were asked to say that Mrs Kirwan's death was accidental! If, apart from the medical evidence, the conduct and demeanour of the prisoner, together with the whole facts and circumstances of the case, left no rational doubt of his guilt, it was their duty to find him guilty.

In charging the jury, Mr Justice Crampton referred to the mantle of mystery spread over the case, and explained the nature and effect of circumstantial evidence. Having reviewed the undisputed facts, his Lordship went through the proof at large. That the parties were not living on good terms as husband and wife was proved by the character and conduct of the prisoner. The testimony of all the medical men was, substantially, that the external injuries could not have been the cause of death. While they found no marks of violence, that did not exclude the mode of destruction suggested by the Crown — the forcible application of the sheet — which the doctors admitted would leave no signs distinguishable from those of drowning. All were agreed that the appearances, external and internal, were consistent with either simple drowning or forcible immersion. Dr Hatchell went further: he thought the congestion greater than could be accounted for by drowning alone. Thus the jury were left by the doctors in a state of much uncertainty. His Lordship then commented on the demeanour of the prisoner on 6 September. The jury would consider whether that was due to genuine grief or was merely affected to avert suspicion. As to the sheet, it was for them to decide which of the Nangles was in error. Both seemed anxious to tell the truth; but it was very dark at the time, a fact which should also be kept in view with reference to the finding of the clothes. Patrick Nangle's account of his being interrupted by Mr Kirwan at the inquest was corroborated by the Coroner. It was admitted that three cries from Ireland's Eye were heard that evening about seven o'clock. If the screams heard by Larkin came from the Long Hole, they must have come across the island, and consequently must have been heard by the prisoner. The credit of the five witnesses who heard these cries was unimpeached. If they were uttered by the deceased lady, what caused them? Undoubtedly, pressing and imminent danger of some kind. Were they the screams of a person seized by epilepsy, or were they due to pain or fear caused by another? The jury would consider whether the character of the cries was consistent with an attack of epilepsy to a person bathing. They would also consider whether this lady, an experienced bather and an expert swimmer, was swimming in 2 feet 9 inches of water when she was seized with epilepsy and gave the screams described. It was impossible that she herself placed the sheet where it was found, as the rock was then covered by water. How came she upon that rock? Was it probable that the tide threw her on it and left her there? Again, did she ever in her life have an epileptic fit? Suspicion must not be confounded with evidence. But if they could not reconcile these facts with the prisoner's innocence, they must not pass them over; if, on the other hand, they were not satisfied that Mrs Kirwan's death was the result of violence, they would acquit him.

At seven o'clock the jury retired to consider their verdict.

Returning in forty minutes, they intimated that they could not agree, and the Court adjourned till eleven o'clock. On its reassembling, however, the jury were no further forward, and it was proposed to lock them up all night and to take their verdict in the morning. They asked for a little more time, and wished to hear Dr Adams repeat his testimony, but the judge supposed that gentleman was then fast asleep; he gave them his own recollection of the Doctor's evidence: that death might have been caused by either simple or forcible drowning. The jury then said they were likely to agree, and in fifteen minutes arrived at a verdict of guilty.[17] The Court adjourned.

When the Court met next day to pronounce sentence, Mr Butt moved that certain questions of law be reserved for the decision of the Court of Criminal Appeal, namely, whether the evidence of the prisoner having lived at Sandymount with a woman who called herself "Mrs Kirwan" was admissible; whether the verdict was founded on the testimony of Dr Adams, a witness for the defence; and whether the deposition of the prisoner at the inquest ought to have been admitted? The Court refused the application. Asked what he had to say why sentence of death should not be passed against him, the prisoner, "in a firm and perfectly calm voice", entered at length upon a discussion of the evidence. As he made no fresh statement and merely repeated the facts known to everyone in Court, Mr Justice Crampton said:

> I am sorry to interrupt you at this painful moment, but you must be well aware that your counsel entered into all these subjects. It is impossible for me now to go into the evidence.

His Lordship then pronounced sentence of death, intimating his own concurrence and that of his learned brother in the rightness of the verdict, and pointing out that there was no hope of pardon on this side of the grave. The prisoner, again

[17] It would seem from the letter before cited, written by the Foreman "on behalf of himself and ten of the Jury," that this trouble was due to the obstinacy of one intransigent juror. How he came to be converted by the doubtful opinion of Dr Adams does not appear.

protesting his innocence, was removed under escort to Kilmainham Jail, and the Court rose.

The Official Report of the trial concludes: "By order of the Executive Government the sentence was commuted to transportation for life." This result was achieved by the joint endeavours of the Rev. J. A. Malet, who produced, anonymously, the brochure before cited,[18] and of J. Knight Boswell, a Dublin solicitor, who published a pamphlet on similar lines.[19] Both tracts give an *ex parte* review of the evidence and contain a series of declarations by divers persons, more or less relevant to the issue, as to which it may be generally observed that such irresponsible pronouncements, not upon oath, are plainly of less value than statements sworn to in court. I have space but to glance at this new "evidence".

The Kirwan Case crop includes Mrs Crowe, the mother of Mrs Kirwan, who said she was in constant touch with her daughter and that Mr Kirwan was always a most kind, affectionate husband. She makes no reference to the Sandymount establishment, and as regards her daughter's health condescends only upon sleeplessness; she does not mention fits. Her daughter was "very venturesome in the water, going into the deep parts of the sea, and continuing therein for a much longer period than other ladies".[20] Mrs Bentley said that she knew the deceased intimately. Mrs Kirwan became aware of the Kenny connection within a month of her marriage, and "exhibited no emotion on the subject". Two years before, she told the declarant that she had a fit in presence of her husband. Two other ladies severally averred that Patrick Nangle had equivocated about the sheet, and had expressed an intention to "pinch" Mr Kirwan at the trial. There follows a certificate by ten Dublin physicians

---

[18] *The Kirwan Case.*
[19] *Defence of William Bourke Kirwan, condemned for the alleged Murder of his Wife, and now a Convict in Spike-Island: to which, amongst other documents, is appended the Opinion of Alfred S. Taylor, M.D., F.R.S., the most eminent medico-legal writer in the Empire, that "No murder was committed".* Dublin: Printed by Webb and Chapman, Great Brunswick Street. 1853.
[20] Yet Mr Malet avers that she "could not swim at all". — *The Kirwan Case.*

and surgeons, proceeding upon the "sworn testimony annexed", that the appearances were "quite compatible with death caused by simple drowning or by seizure of a fit in the water"; and that they were given to understand that Mrs Kirwan's father died of a fit eight years ago".[21] The great Dr Taylor wrote on 20 December 1852, denouncing the verdict: we shall hear his opinion presently. Anne Maher, Kirwan's servant, said that two years before Mrs Kirwan had a fit in the presence of her husband and one Kelly. Arthur Kelly said he had been Kirwan's "assistant" for twelve years; he assisted at two fits, one two years ago and another in June last, just before Mrs Kirwan left for Howth. *Neither of these declarations was upon oath;* Anne Maher could not write.[22] An uncle and a cousin of the deceased said that she often complained of blood to the head and "confusion of ideas"; adding with delightful if unconscious humour that she spoke in the highest praise of her husband's conduct and "always appeared in the full and affluent enjoyment of comfort and respectability". Mr Butt wrote to say that the epileptic theory was not thought of till the second day of the trial, when it was suggested by a medical witness, too late to call evidence in its support — as though he had not had an opportunity of consulting his own client! The remaining volunteers allege that Kirwan had nothing to do with choosing the wet grave, that the Crown expert's measurements at the Long Hole were defective, that the acoustics of the island were other than as represented, and that Mrs Kirwan had once told a servant, with reference to a little boy who came to the house enquiring for "dada", "that it was Mr Kirwan's son, and he had two or three more of them." Here endeth *The Kirwan Case.*

Islands would seem to have exercised a baleful influence

[21] These gentlemen had not the advantage of inspecting the body or of hearing the evidence. The "testimony" on which they rely was, as we shall see, *not* "sworn". It is also to be noted that Mrs Crowe says nothing about the manner of her husband's death.

[22] This is the "sworn testimony" which weighed with the ten physicians. It is remarkable that Mr Kirwan omitted at the inquest to mention these seizures, and that he did not instruct his counsel to adduce at the trial evidence of such importance.

upon Mr Kirwan's fortunes. Fatal, in any view of his behaviour, were the hours spent by him upon Ireland's Eye; and now His Excellency the Earl of Eglinton, the Lord-Lieutenant, whether dissenting from the verdict, or impressed by these declarations, or yielding merely to popular clamour, commuted the sentence to penal servitude for life, and the convict was immured accordingly on Spike Island in Queenstown harbour.[23]

In the other pamphlet[24] Mr Boswell discusses the controversial points of the case, and publishes among certain statements a declaration by Teresa Kenny. But the second "Mrs Kirwan" is disappointing: she was plainly in no mood for revelations. She very handsomely accepts sole responsibility for the *liaison*, of which she alleges the wife was all along aware, and says that in 1848 Mr Kirwan urged her to go to her brother in America, a proposition declined by her in the spirit of Ruth's refusal to forsake Naomi. She was unable to bear witness at the trial, having cut her thumb. Since her protector's arrest, she and her children had suffered much persecution at the hands of the righteous. But what the testimony of Teresa lacks in sensation is amply atoned for by the statement that on 6 September there was upon the island another man, one John Gorman, who avouched "that Kirwan was as innocent of the murder as the child unborn"! Unfortunately this person, having unbosomed himself to Mr Malet, absconded, alleging, with some show of reason, that "he was afraid of being implicated himself", and no trace of him could be found. So the pamphlet is not enriched by his declaration which, like "an affidavit from a thunderstorm or a few words on oath from a heavy shower", desiderated by a certain Chancellor, was not forthcoming. Mr Boswell has a stronger hand to play in Dr Taylor. That forensic autocrat had contributed to the medical press an article, reprinted at length in the pamphlet.[25] As this is not a medical

---

[23] An interesting account of life in that place of involuntary retreat may be read in *The Nunquam Papers* by Mr Robert Blatchford, 1891.

[24] *Defence of William Bourke Kirwan.*

[25] "Considerations on the Medical Evidence of Death from Drowning, in relation to the case of William B. Kirwan." By Alfred S. Taylor, M.D., F.R.S. — *Dublin Quarterly Journal of Medical Science,* February, 1853.

journal and not all my readers are medical jurists, I do not propose to accompany Dr Taylor in his pathological excursus. Those professionally interested may read him for themselves. His conclusions are as follows:

> I assert as my opinion, from a full and unbiassed examination of the medical evidence in this case, that so far as the appearances of the body are concerned, there is an entire absence of proof that death was the result of violence at the hands of another. Persons while bathing, or exposed to the chance of drowning, are often seized with fits which may prove suddenly fatal, although they may allow of a short struggle; the fit may arise from syncope, apoplexy, or epilepsy. Either of the last conditions would, in my opinion, reconcile all the medical circumstances of this remarkable case.

While admitting the force of the moral and circumstantial evidence against the accused, Dr Taylor holds that, "looking at the unsatisfactory nature of the medical evidence of violent death, it would certainly have justified a verdict of Not Proven".

The Doctor, however, was not to have it all his own way. There was published by Professor Geoghegan the result of *his* examination of the same facts, which led him to a very different conclusion.[26] The copy of this pamphlet now before me is interesting as having been presented by the author to Mr Smyly, QC, who conducted the prosecution. Why that learned counsel did not put the Professor in the box is an additional mystery.[27] To me, a layman in such matters, Dr Geoghegan's arguments upon the medical evidence seem much more cogent and convincing than those of Dr Taylor. His summing up is as follows:

[26] *An Examination of the Medical Facts in the Case of the Queen* v. *W. B. Kirwan.* By Thomas G. Geoghegan, M.D., Fellow and Professor of Forensic Medicine, Royal College of Surgeons, Ireland: Surgeon to the City of Dublin Hospital, and the Hospital for Incurables; Hon. Memb. Nat. Hist. Soc. Montreal, etc., etc. Dublin: J. Fannin & Co., 41 Grafton Street. 1853.

[27] The chief medical witness for the prosecution, as appears, had not risen to his precognition: "Dr Hatchell's testimony, I will admit, did not come up to what the Crown had been led to believe and expect." — Mr Hayes' address to the jury.

The preceding considerations, I think, suffice to indicate that the entire series of medical facts leads to the following conclusions: (1) That the death of Mrs Kirwan was not the result of apoplexy, or of epilepsy, nor yet of epileptic or of suicidal drowning. (2) That the combined conditions of the body (both external and internal) were incompatible with drowning, unattended by other violence. (3) That the appearances observed may have been produced by strangulation alone, or combined with compression of the chest, or with partial smothering. (4) That they are also consistent with a combination of the preceding mixed or simple process of strangulation, with drowning; the submersion not having been continuous from its commencement.[28]

That Dr Geoghegan was in the better position to form a judgment would appear from the following circumstances: he had been consulted by the Crown at an early stage of the case, had personally inspected the *locus*, and heard the whole trial, none of which advantages was enjoyed by Dr Taylor. Further, he ascertained from witnesses who had seen the body certain conditions not elicited in evidence. From observations made by him at the Long Hole, Dr Geoghegan believed that the deed was done at the landward side of the "body" rock, in shallow water; the presence of seaweed and gravel in the hair favoured that view, and there would be less chance of detection from the wetting of the perpetrator's clothes. "The arrangement of the deceased's bathing-dress, and of the sheet beneath her, with the orderly position of the body, seem clearly to shew that wherever death may have occurred, the corpse was placed subsequently on the rock."[29]

Actuated as I always am by a laudable desire to give the reader full value for his money, and believing that the opinion of a modern authority on forensic medicine might prove helpful, I consulted, unprofessionally, my friend Dr Devon, who was so good as to make a careful study of the whole medical phenomena, and to favour me with his conclusions.

[28] *An Examination of the Medical Facts*, etc.
[29] *An Examination of the Medical Facts*, etc.

Of the competency of Dr Devon to pronounce upon the question it would be impertinent to speak.[30] His report is too long for quotation here, and I must be content to quote one pregnant paragraph:

> In this case it was suggested that deceased had an apoplectic stroke; but there was no evidence in the brain of any haemorrhage. Syncope was also put forward as a cause of death; but the appearances found pointed to death from asphyxia. Epilepsy was also advanced as a cause, with as little evidence to support it. Granting however that deceased fell into the water from an epileptic or a fainting fit, and there was drowned, how could she have sustained the injuries she had received and be found lying on her back? If she had fallen forward against projecting rocks or stones, might she not have cut her face and breast and bruised her right side? Possibly; but if she fell *forward* and got injured and drowned, how did she fall *backward* on a sheet, with her clothes up under her armpits? I am unable to imagine any accidental or suicidal drowning in which the deceased would be found in the position and with the injuries of Mrs Kirwan. And how might it have occurred? If the sheet on which she was found lying had been put round her when she was alive, in some such way as it was put round her dead body before it was removed, she could easily have been submerged in shallow water. If she had been shoved from behind, the injuries might have been received from the rocks or stones in the bed of the water. There was no evidence of throttling and there were no injuries on her back. The body seems to have been taken to the place in which it was found, and in the process the clothes might have been drawn up to the armpits. It was a simple murder, clumsily carried out. If the body had been left in the water there would have been less room for suspicion, but it is a common thing for people under emotional stress to get exhausted mentally and to behave with a degree of stupidity that is amazing.

Who shall decide when doctors disagree? Dr Taylor asks "whether any amount of moral evidence can compensate for a

---

[30] James Devon, F.R.F.P.S.G., H.M. Prison Commissioner for Scotland; for eighteen years Medical Officer, H.M. Prison, Glasgow, and Medico-Legal Examiner for the Crown.

deficiency of proof of the cause of death?" But though medical opinion be thus divided, some weight must surely attach to other facts and circumstances indicating foul play, hardly to be reconciled with death from natural causes.[31] If so, the secret of the island would seem to be rather an open one after all, and like the song the Sirens sang, not beyond all conjecture.

A quarter of a century after the trial the following paragraph appeared in the Dublin press:

AN OLD TRAGEDY REVIVED

More than twenty-five years ago a man named Kirwan, who lived in Upper Merrion Street, and had official employment as a draughtsman, was convicted in the Courthouse, Green Street, of the murder of his wife at Ireland's Eye, under circumstances of peculiar atrocity and horror. Sentence of death was pronounced; the gallows was prepared, the hangman retained, and the rope ready for its work; but at the last moment powerful influence of a very special character was successfully exerted, to rescue the culprit from the grasp of the executioner. Kirwan's death sentence was commuted to penal servitude for life, and after a short stay in Mountjoy Prison he was sent to Spike Island, where he spent nearly twenty-four years as a convict. Last week he was liberated, on condition that he should leave the country, and he has sailed, *via* Queenstown, for America. One who saw him just before his departure describes him as an aged and very respectable-looking gentleman, white-haired, bent, and feeble, and with nothing in his aspect or manner to suggest that he was guilty of the awful tragedy on Ireland's Eye.[32]

Some further particulars are furnished by Mr M'Donnell

---

[31] Three years later, in the celebrated Palmer case, where the medical battle was between strychnia and tetanus as the cause of death, Dr Taylor, chief expert for the Crown, failed to find in the body any trace of the strychnia which Professors Herapath and Nunneley maintained must, if administered, have been present. Yet the "moral evidence" of Palmer's guilt turned the scale. As that gentleman himself philosophically remarked, "It was the riding that did it."

[32] *Freeman's Journal*, 3 February 1879.

Bodkin, KC, in his account of the case,[33] on the authority of the late Dr O'Keefe, formerly prison doctor at Spike Island, who "accompanied Kirwan when, on his release, as the last prisoner on Spike Island (before it was turned to its present use), he proceeded to Liverpool, whence he sailed to America, with the intention of joining and marrying the mother of his children, whose name figured so prominently at his trial". A reunion sufficiently remarkable, whatever the view you take of the mystery. The local tradition that a venerable and flowing-bearded stranger, who some years afterwards visited Ireland's Eye and remained wrapped in contemplation of the Long Hole, was Mr Kirwan, surveying the scene of his adventure, may be dismissed as legendary.

---

[33] *Famous Irish Trials*, Dublin: 1918. The list of *errata* appended to this volume, though formidable enough, does not include the learned author's repeated statement that no one reading the evidence can have the faintest doubt of Mr Kirwan's innocence.

The Poisoned Chocolates

H. M. Walbrook

The present author's earliest recollection of the Poisoned Chocolates case dates back to one of the many pleasant evenings spent with the Brighton Musical Fraternity in the late 1890s. The President of the Fraternity in those years was the late Mr Wilhelm Kuhe, the famous pianist and concert-impresario, who, from the days of Jenny Lind to those of Patti, Paderewski, and Clara Butt, brought all the great musical artists of his day to sing or play at Brighton. He was one of the most lovable as well as one of the most picturesque of men, and the nights when he was able to take the chair at the Fraternity meetings in the banqueting-room of the Old Ship Hotel were *noctes notandae*. He always played us something from one of the great masters, and, venerable as he was, played it like a master, and, when his health had been toasted with "musical honours", he always made a delightful speech, rich in wisdom, and reminiscence. On the occasion to which I allude he told us the following story:

A year or two ago I spent part of the Christmas holiday with some friends whose house was in the neighbourhood of a great criminal lunatic asylum. On the evening of my arrival my host and hostess mentioned that it was their custom to go to the Christmas ball at this institution. They asked me if I would care to accompany them, and I replied that it would much interest me to do so. The experience proved extremely curious, and I brought away with me a host of unforgettable impressions. The figure I most vividly remember was that of one of the inmates, a tall woman of more than middle age, who, while dancing, suddenly caught sight of me, and stared hard at me again and again as she waltzed with her partner round the ballroom. When the dance was finished she came straight up to me. "You are Mr Wilhelm Kuhe," she said. "I am," I replied, looking into her face, and

117

observing that it was powdered and painted to an extent that was disgusting. "You don't remember me?" she said with a ghastly smile: her mouth appeared to have been contorted as if by paralysis. I had to admit that I did not. "Have you forgotten all the excitement there was over Christiana Edmunds?" she asked. Then her story came back to me. She was the woman who in the year 1871 sent a thrill through England by distributing poisoned chocolate-creams to children in the streets of Brighton, and who was afterwards charged with murder, tried, and sentenced to death, but was subsequently found to be insane, and committed for the remainder of her life to the Broadmoor Criminal Lunatic Asylum.

There were many in the audience who as they listened to this story remembered the woman's crimes and the sensation they caused, and Mr Kuhe's description of his meeting with her, nearly thirty years after, sent an audible stir through the company.

In its mixture of frivolity and horror the story of Christiana Edmunds is, indeed, hard to parallel. She was born in 1828, at Margate, where her father, an architect and engineer, designed the lighthouse and other public edifices, and died in tragic circumstances in his forty-seventh year. After his death the widow and her children moved to Brighton, where they occupied one of the handsome houses in Gloucester Place, facing the new parish church of St Peter's. In the year 1870 Christiana was the only surviving child. Tall, fair, of graceful figure, always elegantly dressed, cultivated, and a person of very agreeable manners, she had become a familiar figure in the society of the town. Although forty-two years of age she looked much younger, and it was part of her vanity that she gave herself out to be thirty-three. One day, when she was promenading with her mother along the sea-front, a gentleman passed and gave her — probably quite unintentionally — a glance fated to be a turning-point in her life. He was a local physician, married, and with a family of young children; and Miss Edmunds seems to have fallen in love with him there and then. A day or two later she told her mother that she was feeling ill. Meanwhile she had been making inquiries as to the name and address of the attractive promenader, and she now informed Mrs Edmunds that he was a practitioner of exceptional ability and that she wished him to be called in. The mother did as she was desired, and in due course Dr Beard made his appearance at the house in Gloucester Place. It was fated to be the unluckiest call he ever made.

A friendship promptly sprang up between the pair, which rapidly developed on the lady's part into a violent love-affair. She wrote him long and extraordinary letters, addressing him as "Caro mio", ending up with allusions to "long kisses", and signed "Dorothea". At the same time, the doctor duly observed the proprieties by introducing her to his wife, and she became a frequent visitor at his home and apparently the devoted friend of the whole family. That the physician ever actually behaved as a lover to her is most unlikely, but there is no denying that he displayed an indiscretion out of all keeping with the social ethics of his profession. He preserved her letters, and failed on their arrival to show them to his wife. Had he taken that step the visits of Miss Edmunds would no doubt have been terminated in time to avert the tragic events that followed. It is quite likely that Mrs Beard already had her suspicions of her husband's patient, and it is certain that Miss Edmunds inwardly detested "la Sposa", as she called the doctor's wife in her letters, and wanted her "Caro Mio" for herself.

In March 1871, the situation of the three figures in the drama was dramatically laid bare. Miss Edmunds paid one of her visits to the doctor's house, taking with her a box of sweets. She found her hostess alone, and had a pleasant talk with her in the drawing-room, in the course of which she opened the box, took from it a chocolate-cream, extolled its flavour, and playfully put it into her hostess's mouth. Mrs Beard bit it, swallowed some of it, found its taste "horrible", and ejected the rest. Her guest made some light-hearted remark and proffered another, which was declined, and presently bade her an affectionate farewell, leaving Mrs Beard haunted with an unmistakable suspicion which deepened when she subsequently experienced severe pains and sickness.

At first she kept her misgivings to herself. They were, indeed, too grave to be easily put into words. However, a couple of days later, she described the whole incident to her husband, and openly expressed her belief that Miss Edmunds had tried to poison her. On consideration, the doctor took a similar view of the matter, arranged a meeting with Miss Edmunds, communicated to her his wife's allegation, added quite plainly that he believed it to be correct, and ended the conversation by forbidding her to hold any further communication with him or ever enter his home again.

Shaken to the centre, the young woman hurried home. "The doctor has charged me with attempting to murder his wife! Me! Murder! I shall go mad! Oh, I shall go mad!" she said to her mother in a frenzy of rage. The mother's reply was more appalling still. "My poor child," she wailed, bursting into a flood of tears, "you are mad already!" and she proceeded to communicate a secret which hitherto she had kept from her daughter, namely that on both sides of the family there had already been cases of dangerous and incurable insanity. Apparently, however, the sole effect of this communication upon the daughter was to intensify her fury against the friend who had slandered her. "He must withdraw it! There must be an apology!" was her cry; and the more her mother urged that the wiser course under all the circumstances was to say nothing, the more the daughter demanded that her name should be cleared. In the end Mrs Edmunds gave way, and a letter was sent to the doctor threatening proceedings unless the slander was withdrawn and fully apologized for. It remained unanswered. Dr Beard had said all he had to say; he had forbidden his quondam friend the house, and he now took refuge in silence. From that day onward Christiana Edmunds was a desperate woman. She still loved her "Caro Mio", and she now lived with but one object — namely, to prove her innocence, and to convince not only Dr Beard, but if necessary the whole of Brighton, that if there was a poisoner in the town, he or she lived somewhere else than in Gloucester Place.

Rich in cunning was the scheme which she thought out and duly put into operation. Going for one of her afternoon walks in the town, she stopped one of the poor children in the street and, with the promise of a reward, sent him to a well-known sweet-shop to buy her a quantity of chocolate-creams, bidding him to bring them to where she would be waiting for them. The child obeyed, conveyed them to the lady who had paid for them, and was sent away with a copper or two for himself. She then took the chocolates home with her, and, in the seclusion of her bedroom, carefully opened them, injected a quantity of strychnine or arsenic into each, ingeniously closed them up, and put them back into the original paper bag in which the confectioner had packed them. A day or two later she went out again, taking the bag of poisoned sweets with her, and, presently meeting another boy, asked him to take them to the shop and change them for a similar quantity of smaller ones, as the lady who bought them had not ordered such large ones. The boy obeyed. The shop-assistant obligingly changed them, emptied the bag of poisoned articles into the box from which the original ones had been taken, refilled the bag with the smaller delicacies, as desired, and sent the little fellow back to the lady. This operation the amiable shop-assistant allowed to be repeated more than once; and presently people began to say that a certain shopkeeper was dealing death around by selling deleterious sweets!

One victim of them was a boy of four, Sidney Albert Barker by name, who died within twenty minutes of eating one out of a bagful which an uncle had bought for him. At the inquest a lady unknown to the family came forward and volunteered to give evidence. Her story was that she also had known of doubtful sweets being sold at the shop in question and of purchasers being made seriously ill by them. She gave her name as Miss Christiana Edmunds, and her narrative created a great sensation. Among other consequences, it brought an emphatic declaration from the unfortunate shopkeeper that he had never had a complaint before, and that he only bought his goods from the very best firms in the country. Threatened with ruin, he also stated that he had now burnt his entire stock of chocolates, and that he would sell no more. The public-spirited Miss Edmunds had created another thrill in the witness-box by roundly denouncing the local police for their stupidity! She declared that she had personally warned them of what was happening. In short, she came away from the inquest the heroine of the occasion, and as the proceedings were reported at length in the local newspapers, it is extremely likely that Dr Beard read of the courage of the friend he had so wantonly accused of murder. He still, however, withheld his apology for the slander he had uttered against her.

After that the shop scandal stopped, and little Sidney Barker's death soon took its place among the unsolved mysteries of the moment. Presently, however, another and equally alarming development followed. Various residents in the town began to receive, through the post, boxes of cakes, fruit, and sweets, all looking very dainty, and accompanied in each case by a cordial letter, written in an unfamiliar hand, but showing an intimate knowledge of the person or persons to whom it was addressed. It was observed that in several cases the recipients of these little attentions became shortly afterwards seriously ill. In one instance the enclosed communication was worded as follows:

> A few home-made cakes for the children. Those done up are flavoured on purpose for yourself to enjoy. You will guess who this is from. I can't mystify you, I fear. I hope this will arrive for you to-night while the eatables are fresh.

Some of the boxes were posted in Brighton; others came from London; and one of the recipients was the outspoken Miss Edmunds of Gloucester Place, whose revelations had caused such a stir at the inquest on the boy Barker. Once more she went to the Town Hall, told the police what had happened, called upon them for prompt action in the public interest, and frankly addressed them as "idiots".

At last the Chief Constable of the town, Mr George White, drew up an advertisement, which appeared in the *Brighton Daily News* on 17 August, 1871, offering a reward of twenty pounds for any information leading to the apprehension of the mysterious criminal. Among those who happened to read it were the chemists who had been supplying Miss Edmunds with strychnine, and that day her name was confidentially mentioned to Mr White as that of a resident regarding whom he might perhaps with advantage make inquiries. He did so. He was shown some of the letters by which she had gained possession of a large quantity of poison, discovered them to be forgeries, and compared their handwriting with that of letters which from time to time he had received from the lady herself and also of those sent with the boxes of cake and fruit. He also got into communication with Dr Beard. And on 19 August, in the Town Hall police-court, before the local stipendiary and a crowded bench of magistrates, Miss Christiana Edmunds made a startling appearance, not in the witness-box, but in the dock, charged with having attempted to murder the doctor's wife.

The magisterial inquiry went on for weeks, adjourned from Thursday to Thursday, and from beginning to end provided Thackeray's "Cheerful Dr Brighton" with the greatest criminal sensation in its history. The crowd outside before the doors opened, wrote a local journalist, was a sight to break a theatre-manager's heart with envy! The social position of the accused woman, her elegant appearance, and the steadily-accumulating evidence of her wickedness and cunning combined to make her horribly attractive to the public. A pen-and-ink portrait of her was on sale in the streets, and when she was shown a copy of it she evinced considerable indignation. It did her no sort of justice, she said. Otherwise she was outwardly the calmest person in court. On taking her place in the dock at the opening of each day's proceedings she would turn her large, restless eyes on the throng in the public gallery and nod and smile at such friends as she recognized. Even when Dr Beard stepped into the witness-box and told his story of her letters to him and her behaviour to his wife, her features did not relax. As the children whom she had made her accomplices faltered their damning evidence against her she listened to their stories with unruffled calm. In the end she was committed for trial at the forthcoming Winter Assizes at Lewes on the two-fold charge of murdering Sidney Albert

Barker and attempting to murder Mrs Beard, and was conveyed from the Town Hall to the county gaol amid a storm of popular execration. Such, indeed, was the feeling against her all over Sussex that it was felt that a fair trial and an impartial verdict were more than could be expected for her even from a jury of Lewes men, and it was ultimately arranged that her trial should take place in London.

It opened on 15 January, 1872, in the Old Bailey, and lasted two days. The Judge was Sir Samuel Martin, Baron of the Exchequer, an Irishman, very popular both inside and outside the courts, and one whose judgments in criminal cases were equally remarkable for their brevity and leniency, while two distinguished advocates of the day, Serjeant Ballantine and Serjeant Parry, led respectively for the prosecution and the defence. Never was the case of an accused individual more considerately or more humanely handled. Serjeant Ballantine, of course, sketched in detail the story of the prisoner's infatuation for a married man, and of the forgeries by which she had obtained a large part of the poisons she used; but again and again in his speech came little indications that her proceedings had been those of an insane person; while Serjeant Parry, in his eloquent speech for the defence, made her lunacy his sole plea for her pardon.

The most dramatic episode of the whole trial, however, came with the entry into the witness-box of the prisoner's mother. Dreadful was the story she poured forth in a voice half choked with sobs. Clad in mourning and bowed with sorrow, Mrs Edmunds described to the court a family "saturated with lunacy". The prisoner's father, she said, had died in Earlswood Asylum in his forty-seventh year. The prisoner's brother had died in another asylum. The prisoner's sister had attempted to commit suicide by throwing herself from a window. The witness's own father had been an imbecile during the last years of his life, and had died in an epileptic fit; and the daughter of one of her brothers had been similarly afflicted. As the weeping woman faltered forth this awful recital there was not a dry eye in the court, and a sudden breakdown of the prisoner in sobs completed the piteousness of the scene. Every word that Mrs Edmunds had spoken was true, but how great was the courage that gave such a picture to the world! Seldom, surely, has a mother made a braver and more self-sacrificing effort to save a child from unmerited disaster than Mrs Edmunds made in the witness-box that day.

Even in London's Central Criminal Court, however, the prejudice against the accused was too great for mercy to be able to temper justice. The Judge, with his customary fairness, gave due weight in his charge to the jury to the plea of lunacy, but significantly added that the prisoner seemed to have been quite aware of the wickedness of her acts and of the likelihood of their consequences; and in the end the jury returned a verdict of Guilty. On being asked if she had any reason to offer why sentence should not be pronounced, the prisoner replied in a low but clear voice: "It is owing to my having been Dr Beard's patient that I have been brought into this position. I wish the jury could have known the exact particulars of his intimacy with me, and the way I have been treated." She further declared herself to be pregnant with a quick child. On hearing this the Judge immediately ordered the empanelling of a jury of matrons to examine her, and she was removed from the court. On this jury being brought back, their forewoman declared that they had found the prisoner's allegation to be false. After that she was sentenced to death.

Next day the newspapers reflected the contrasted passions of anger and pity which the case had kindled. The *Brighton Daily News* openly rejoiced in the verdict, and its leading article on the subject concluded as follows: "Better that a dozen mad murderers should be hanged than one sane murderer should escape, for, after all, what is death to an insane person? If, in spite of all our care, a really insane person should be put to death, there would be little reason to grieve for one who had been delivered from a world of illusions cruel to himself and dangerous to all around." Such an argument strikes one today as monstrous; but it reflected the horror with which a series of reckless crimes was still locally regarded. In London, the *Daily Telegraph* took the opposite line. In an equally plain-spoken leader, that journal, then at the height of its power as a voice of the people, stigmatized both the verdict and the sentence as thoroughly discreditable. "If," declared the writer, "this wretched, half-crazed creature, the sister, daughter, and grandchild of lunatics, is put out of the world in deference to a judicial definition of the plea of insanity, her death will bring disgrace upon British justice."

Fortunately this latter opinion prevailed. The Judge communicated with the Home Secretary, who considered the whole case, and ultimately tendered his advice to the Queen that the sentence should be commuted to one of committal for life to an asylum. Her Majesty's consent was speedily forthcoming, and Christiana Edmunds was removed to Broadmoor, where she spent the remainder of her life. She died in 1907 in her seventy-ninth year. And the picture given of her by Mr Kuhe shows that she retained her vivacity and her vanity to the end of her long life. Today her melancholy story is recalled dispassionately as an outstanding case not only of the cunning of the insane, but of the risks of lunatic ancestry. It is also perhaps remembered as a warning to married professional gentlemen whose clients address them as "Caro Mio" to show the letters promptly to their wives and close the correspondence.

Matricide at the Metropole

Jonathan Goodman

Sidney Harry Fox, Rosaline Fox's fourth and last and favourite child, was born in the Norfolk village of Great Fransham in January 1899. Whether he was the son of Mr Fox, who was a train signalman, or of Rosaline's lover, a porter on the same line, is not clear, but he certainly grew up with ideas above his station. His belief that he was of noble origin seems to have formed the foundation of a confidence that enabled him, despite an unprepossessing appearance (his form was runtish, his hair crinkly, his eyes obtrusive), to ape aristocracy and wealthiness in the furtherance of fraud; the same belief may have nurtured what became, by his early twenties, an unblemished amorality that allowed him to dismiss work as something to occupy the time of the lower classes, and to assess individuals in terms of the ease with which they might be bilked.

Unfortunately, so far as Fox was concerned, his quite considerable talent both as an impersonator of chequebook-holders and as an imitator of their signatures was offset by stupidity. His planning rarely extended farther than the deception; afterwards, his main hope of evading retribution lay in the clarity of his guilt, which suggested that he was unpractised in the ways of crime and therefore provided certain of his victims with the excuse to give him "one more chance". Others of his prey, with whom he had mixed homosexual pleasure with business, preferred to accept their losses and say nothing.

But not all of Fox's victims found excuses or reasons for letting him off scot-free, and between 1918 and 1928 he received half a dozen prison sentences, the last and longest being for fifteen months. His mother — described by F. Tennyson Jesse as "the old, white-haired woman with the big, genial face, and the loose, smiling lips, the shuffling gait [she suffered from *paralysis agitans*], and the trembling hands"[1] — was always waiting for him when he was released, and to her he always returned. They spent some of his free time in cheap furnished rooms in and around London and on the south coast; and when they desired a little luxury, they stayed in hotels, invariably flitting without paying for their keep.

In 1927, Mrs Fox struck up a friendship with a Mrs Morse, the middle-aged wife of a captain in the Merchant Navy who was then in the Far East, and the two women took a flat at Southsea, the resort-town proximate to Portsmouth. Soon afterwards, Sidney joined them; and soon after that, turning his talent for impersonation to heterosexuality, he made Mrs Morse believe that he was in love with her, and then took out an insurance policy on her life and persuaded her to make a will in his favour. Before many of the weekly premiums had been paid, Mrs Morse awoke one night to find her room filling with gas. Subsequent investigation revealed the source of the fumes as a tap that (a) was hidden by a heavy chest of drawers, (b) could not be turned on except purposely. From then, it seems, Mrs Morse doubted the sincerity of Sidney's loving words and deeds. He, in turn, was saddened by her suspicions, and took his mother to other lodgings; before leaving, however, he helped himself to some of Mrs Morse's jewellery. It was for this theft that he received the prison sentence of fifteen months.

His first action when he came out of prison in March 1929 was to collect his mother from the workhouse where she was staying. On 21 April, Rosaline Fox made a will in which she left everything to Sidney. At that time, "everything" did not amount to much more than the clothes on her back, which included one stockinette dress worn over another; she did not even possess a nightgown. But a week or so after the will was made, her sole legatee increased her post-mortem value to a little over £2000 by taking out the first of two accident policies on her life.

[1] *Trial of Sidney Fox*, William Hodge & Co., Edinburgh, 1934.

Meanwhile, acting on the principle that it is better to travel fraudulently than to arrive, the Foxes, mother and son, had embarked on what turned out to be their final odyssey: a traipsing from one hotel to another in south-east England, living in style for a few days and departing as soon as the respective management began to press for payment. Sidney used a simple method of allaying the qualms of hoteliers when he and his mother first turned up at a reception-counter; after explaining that their luggage was being sent on, he would produce a brown-paper parcel — containing nothing more precious than brown paper — and ask for it to be kept in the safe; this, he delicately implied, was instead of a deposit. Occasionally, he felt the need to make an ostentatious display of a chequebook (someone else's, of course) or a wallet made to bulge by being stuffed with offcuts of the invaluable brown paper; and he might drop a hint that both he and his mummy had private means.

Actually, to be fair to Sidney, his references to private means were exaggerations rather than downright lies. The Foxes, between them, collected an honest eighteen shillings each week — a pension of ten shillings going to Rosaline in recompense for the death of a son during the Great War, and a smaller pension going to Sidney in respect of a slight epileptic condition that was thought to have been aggravated during a brief period in the army which had been forced on him by a victim who offered a choice between military service and penal servitude.

On Wednesday, 16 October 1929, the Foxes arrived at the Hotel Metropole, on the sea-front at Margate, Kent, having come by bus from Canterbury, where they had resided for four nights at the County Hotel; prior to their stay in the cathedral city, they had given their expensive custom to, among other Kentish hostelries, the Royal Pavilion, Folkestone (leaving an unpaid bill of £15.5.0d), and the Grand at Dover (unexcessively fleeced to the tune of £3.5.6d).

Miss Vera Hopper, the receptionist at the Metropole, was quite taken in by the Fox double-act. (Unlike the manager, Joseph Harding, who — so he afterwards claimed — suspected the Foxes of being itinerant rogues when he first clapped eyes on them, and made sure that their account was rendered daily, though not that it was paid.) Vera Hopper considered them so trustworthy that, when they had been staying at the hotel a couple of days, she offered Fox the loan of her own fur coat for his mother's use.[2] Miss Hopper allotted rooms 68 and 70 to the Foxes. These rooms, though adjoining, had no communicating door. Neither of them contained a gas-fire.

Fox's salient actions during the few days preceding his mother's demise can be presented in diary-form:

Friday, 18 October. He travelled to the nearby town of Ramsgate, and paid two shillings for a short-term insurance policy which entitled him to £1000 in the event of his mother's death from external, accidental means.

Sunday, 20 October. He expressed concern about his mother's health to Joseph Harding, who arranged for her to be moved to room No. 66, which had a gas-fire, and for Fox to occupy the adjoining room, No. 67; there was a communicating door between these rooms.

Monday, 21 October. Fox went to a chemist's shop to obtain a tonic that had been prescribed for his mother and — more important — to persuade the assistant to accept a cheque, signed "Rosaline Fox", for two pounds. (Perhaps needless to say, the cheque was subsequently returned by the bank, marked "no account".) Later that day, he used part of the change from the cheque to buy a railway ticket to London.

Tuesday, 22 October. Having stayed overnight in London, he visited the offices of the two companies insuring his mother's life, and arranged for both policies, each of which was about to lapse, to be extended to midnight of the following day; then he returned to Margate.

It appears that while he had been away, Mrs Fox had remained in her room. However, on Wednesday evening, after

---

[2] The fact that the ever-acquisitive Sidney declined the offer of the pawnable fur coat receives no comment in any of the accounts of the case that I have seen; but it is surely a strong indication that he was determined that his mother should not leave the hotel wearing anything cosier than a shroud.

telling the barmaid at the hotel, "Mother and I have had a sham fight, which shows that she is well," he brought her down to the restaurant, where she ate a hearty dinner.

After escorting her back to her room, he went out to get her a half-bottle of port, for which he actually paid. This was either his last act of kindness to his mother or one of the final components of his plan to murder her and still be considered a loving son; or perhaps, since few remarkable actions by someone premeditating murder can be ascribed to a single motive, he was killing two birds with one stone.

Later, round about ten o'clock, he came down to the bar for a quick drink. On his way out of the bar, he caught sight of the manager and reacted very strangely indeed, staring at Mr Harding "as if he had seen a ghost" and then scampering upstairs.

At 11.40 p.m., just twenty minutes before the insurances were due to expire, Sidney entered the lounge and was espied by Samuel Hopkins, a commercial traveller who was staying at the hotel.

There is a story about Dr Johnson, which has it that he was cuddling a lady-friend when his housekeeper entered the room without knocking. "Doctor, I'm *surprised*!" she exclaimed; to which the doctor retorted that the appropriate word was "shocked" — it was he who was surprised. One cannot say whether Samuel Hopkins was surprised or shocked by his first sight of Sidney Fox; but whatever the feeling, it was occasioned by the fact that the young man was wearing naught but a shirt. Hopkin's surprise or shock was soon appended with puzzlement, for Sidney, who gave the impression of being greatly agitated, enquired the whereabouts of the Metropole's boot-boy. While Hopkins was pondering an apparently obsessional anxiety concerning footwear, Sidney changed the subject by commenting: "I believe there is a fire."

Having shouted alarmingly, Hopkins followed Sidney up the stairs and along the corridor to room No. 66. Sidney pointed to the door and cried: "My mother is in there!" Dense black smoke belched into the corridor as Hopkins opened the door. He attempted to walk into the room, but was driven

Mrs Rosaline Fox

back; then, noticing that there was clear air close to the floor, he got down on his hands and knees and groped his way to the bed. His hands came in contact with Mrs Fox's legs, which were dangling over the edge of the bed, and he somehow managed to drag the heavy old woman out of the room. Mrs Fox was naked except for a short vest, and before Hopkins collapsed, he took off his raincoat and threw it over her. As he lapsed into unconsciousness, he heard Fox murmuring: "My mummy . . . my mummy. . . ."

By this time, two more commercial travellers had arrived. They tried to get into room No. 66 through the door that communicated with Fox's room. One of them quickly retreated, but the other, Reginald Reed, succeeded in pulling a burning armchair into the corridor; he then went back into the room and dragged out a patch of burning carpet that had been directly beneath the chair.

While various guests and employees of the hotel sought to

Fox in the Chamber of Horrors
(When first displayed, the effigy was wearing Fox's Old-Etonian tie,
somehow procured by Madame Tussaud's. But after an Old Etonian
visitor to the Chamber complained that Fox was not a fellow-
alumnus, the tie was replaced by the one shown.)

extinguish the flames from the armchair and the patch of
carpet, Sidney stood, unselfconscious in his shirt, on the
outskirts of the crowd; he was seen to wring his hands and was
heard to utter sad sentiments about his mummy.

She, poor woman, was carried down to the entrance hall,
where an attempt was made to revive her by means of artificial
respiration. The doctor who was called soon put a stop to this,
however, for it was clear to him that Rosaline Fox was dead.
And after hearing an account of the fire in room No. 66, the
doctor was equally clear as to the cause of death. He allowed
the appropriately grief-stricken (and by now decently attired)
son to touch the body, and then informed him that his mother
had died from accidental suffocation.

That diagnosis, lacking any autoptic confirmation, was
elongated into a ritual verdict at the inquest that was held next

day, and Sidney Fox, having been issued with a death certificate to go with the insurance policies, popped round to the nearest solicitor, who had no hesitation in advancing him forty pounds on the strength of his prospects. He stayed at the Hotel Metropole one more night, then left, without paying the bill.

The body of Rosaline Fox was buried at Great Fransham on Tuesday, 29 October. The reader may feel that it is redundant to mention that the undertaker's account was never settled. But, for once, Sidney deserves the benefit of the doubt: perhaps he really did intend to pay this bill, and was only prevented from doing so by the fact that he was in police custody by the time the account was rendered.

On 3 November he was arrested at an hotel in Norwich and taken back to Margate to face six charges of fraud upon hotels in Kent, including the Metropole. These, however, were merely "holding charges". Investigators for the insurance companies had learned a number of suspicious facts concerning the death of Rosaline Fox (one of the investigators, after only a short time in Margate, had wired his head office, "Extremely muddy water in this business"), and the companies had got in touch with Scotland Yard. Chief Inspector Walter Hambrook — who, some years before, had arrested Fox for a minor offence — was sent to Margate to make inquiries, and within hours of his arrival felt justified in asking for an order for the exhumation and examination of the body of Mrs Fox. Sir Bernard Spilsbury, the pathologist who carried out the autopsy, concluded that death was due, not to suffocation, but to strangulation.

The grand jury returned a true bill against Fox on the charges of fraud; but when he faced the Margate magistrates on 9 January 1930, a different charge was read:

"That on 23 October 1929, you, Sidney Harry Fox, did feloniously, wilfully, and with malice aforethought kill and murder Rosaline Fox at the Hotel Metropole, Paradise Street, in the parish of St John the Baptist, Margate, in the County of Kent."

"It is absolutely untrue," he claimed. "I deny every word of it."

But at the close of the proceedings he was committed for trial. Because the Kent Assizes had just ended, it was decided that he should stand trial at the impending Sussex Assizes, and so he appeared before Mr Justice Rowlatt in the pretty courthouse at Lewes on 10 March. The prosecution was presented by Sir William Jowitt, who was Attorney-General, and Sir Henry Curtis Bennett; the defence was led by James Dale Cassels.

The case against Fox was virtually watertight; items of evidence, individually strong, were conjoined with others to create impressive overall strength. The evidence of Sir Bernard Spilsbury, which was the weakest part of the case, was invested with ersatz strength, fooling the jurors, by the fact that it was given by Sir Bernard Spilsbury. Ever since his appearance at the trial of Dr Crippen, the press, unmindful of the effect on justice, had written him up as an infallible being; the public — the pool from which jurors were picked — had been brainwashed to believe that Sir Bernard (or "Saint Bernard", as a few sceptics called him) was never wrong. In the Fox case, though his opinion of the cause of death was almost certainly correct, the reasons he gave for arriving at it were inadequate; at the end of his cross-examination by James Cassels, he was forced to admit that "in his experience of strangulation cases, he had never known a case with fewer signs than this".

But despite the deficiencies in the medical evidence, and though the perfect timing of Rosaline Fox's death in relation to the expiry of the insurance policies might be ascribed to coincidence, there remained ample testimony to support a conviction. Any attempt by the defence to show that Mrs Fox — a non-smoker, incidentally — might have died by accident was countered by observations made in room No. 66 following the fire: for instance, that the strip of carpet between the lighted gas-fire and the position of the blazing armchair was unharmed, thus disposing of the notion that the fire was caused by "spitting"; that a mass of charred newspapers found near the spot where the armchair had stood bore the plain inference that they had been intentionally ignited; that a cane chair, situated far away from the area of the fire, was partly burned —

indicating that someone apart from Mrs Fox had been present when the fire started and had moved the chair away, preventing further damage to it.

Some day, an academic person will publish a quite unnecessary monograph explaining that the strength of evidence does not invariably depend on the intellectual quality of the evidence. And, almost certainly, the writer will cite an exchange during the cross-examination of Sidney Fox, after Fox had stated that, at about twenty minutes to midnight on 23 October, he had opened the communicating door to his mother's room, seen a fire blazing, and shut the door before running downstairs for help.

> The Attorney-General: Did you realize, when you opened the communicating door, that the atmosphere in the room was such as would probably suffocate anybody inside?
> A.   If I had stayed there three or four minutes, I should have been suffocated.
> Q.   So you must have been greatly apprehensive for your mother?
> A.   I was.
> Q.   Fox, you closed the door?
> A.   It is quite possible I did.
> Q.   Can you explain to me why it was that you closed the door instead of flinging it wide open?
> A.   *My explanation for that now is that the smoke should not spread into the hotel.*

Even if there had been no true evidence against Fox, the jury might have felt obliged to send him to the scaffold on the basis of that answer alone. But, by then, the verdict was a foregone conclusion. The sole surprise at the end of the nine-day trial was that the jury stayed out of court, presumably deliberating, for as long as an hour and a half.

Room No. 66 at the Hotel Metropole was refurbished in time for the Easter-holiday rush. Several occupants spoke to Joseph Harding, not too complainingly, of things that went bump in the night. It seems that, after Tuesday, 8 April, the day of the execution in Maidstone Gaol, the bumps became, if not louder, more diverse — signifying to the superstitious that Rosaline and Sidney were spiritually together again, the former forgiving, the latter ostensibly contrite. In 1947, the Metropole was demolished in the cause of road-widening. Subsequent bumps in one of Margate's unlicensed guest-houses seeded a tale that the ghostly Foxes had found a new lair; but the tale must be discredited, I think, if only on the ground that the establishment, lacking a single star of recognition, was nowhere near grand enough to attract their custom.

The Bones of Brandy Cove

Richard Whittington-Egan

They lay, gleaming strangely white in the dusky twilight of the late December's afternoon, on the polished surface of an oaken table — a pathetic little heap of human bones.

Christmas was just eleven days away, but there was nothing festive in the atmosphere of the coroner's court at Gowerton, Glamorgan, that day in 1961.

For nearly eight hours, the coroner and his seven-man jury had been trying to find the answer to a grim riddle. Was it possible that here in that small bundle of crumbling bones lay the answer to a question which for forty-two years had mystified the whole of Britain. . . . Where is Mamie Stuart?

Today, the question most people would ask is: *Who* was Mamie Stuart? But back in 1920, everybody knew the name of the twenty-six-year-old ex-chorus girl who seemed to have dissolved into thin air.

Mamie, the daughter of James Stuart, master mariner of Sunderland, had met, on 3 July 1917, a thirty-seven-year-old marine surveyor of Penarth, Cardiff, Everard George Shotton. The couple fell in love and, on 25 March 1918, were married at South Shields register office.

There was, although Mamie did not know it at the time, just one — or rather, two — small flies in the ointment. Shotton already had a wife, whom he had married twelve years before at Newport, and a small son. In blissful ignorance of these impedimenta, Mamie bore her new husband home to Sunderland and triumphantly introduced him to her family.

It was in February 1919 that George and Mamie went to live in Swansea, where, as Mr and Mrs Shotton, they took furnished rooms in the house of a couple named Hearn, at 28 Trafalgar Terrace.

Five months later, on 19 July, Mr Shotton left Trafalgar

Terrace, explaining that his job was taking him away from
Swansea for a while. And on 22 July, Mr and Mrs Hearn saw
Mamie off from Victoria Street station. She was, she told
them, going to spend a short holiday with her parents in
Sunderland.

The Hearns never saw her again. Mrs Hearn had a letter
from her from Sunderland in September 1919, and that, so far
as they were concerned, was the last of Mamie Shotton.

In fact, Mamie returned to Swansea on 5 November 1919.
Shotton met her train, which arrived from Sunderland shortly
before midnight, and took her to the furnished house which he
had rented for six months. Situated close to the village of
Newton, in a pretty seaside area called the Mumbles, 5½ miles
south-west of Swansea, it was a detached two-storey villa,
standing on the top of a hill commanding a magnificent view
of Swansea Bay, and was named Ty-Llanwydd, which means
"The Abode of Peace".

Exactly a week after her arrival, Mamie wrote a letter to her
sister, Mrs Brass. That same day she wrote a letter-card to her
mother and father — posted at Swansea, 5.15 p.m., 12
November.

But when, a few days later, they wrote back to her at
Ty-Llanwydd, their letter was returned to them by the Post
Office, marked "House closed". Puzzled, the Stuarts promptly
despatched a reply-paid telegram to their daughter. This too
was returned, marked "House closed".

Puzzlement turned to alarm.

Then, just before Christmas 1919, a telegram was delivered
at the Stuarts' home at Sunderland. It had been handed in at
Swansea, purported to come from Mamie, and brought them
"the compliments of the season".

The New Year arrived. Still no news. January . . . February
. . . then, in March 1920, came the first confirmation of the
Stuart family's steadily increasing fears.

The manager of the Grosvenor Hotel at Swansea asked the
police to examine a portmanteau which had been left for some
months unclaimed at his hotel. When they opened it, they
found that it contained a second, mutilated, portmanteau, in

which were two dresses, cut to shreds, a pair of lady's boots, also cut to pieces, some small items of personal jewellery, a bible, a rosary, and a manicure set.

It contained, too, a fragment of paper on which was written a Sunderland address.

Inquiries at Sunderland soon established that the address was that of Captain and Mrs Stuart, and when the police went to see them they were informed that the whereabouts of Mamie had been a mystery since the previous December.

The mystery was further complicated by the circumstance that although the portmanteau found at the Grosvenor contained clothing which had undoubtedly belonged to the missing girl, it could in no way be associated with her, for so far as the manager could remember, the bag was left behind by a man who had stayed at the hotel by himself.

Mid-March brought another sinister pointer. A local charwoman, a Mrs Bevan, engaged to clean up Ty-Llanwydd in preparation for new tenants, discovered a mildewed, brown-leather handbag behind the wash-stand in the front bedroom. In it was a sugar ration-card in the name of Mamie Stuart, together with cash amounting to about two pounds.

Weighing all these clues and circumstances, Chief Inspector William Draper of Scotland Yard, who had been called in to help the local force with the investigation, made no bones about the fact that he felt certain that what they were dealing with was a case of murder.

He was equally sure that George Shotton, who by this time was safely back in the arms of his family, living with his legal wife and child at an isolated house named Grey Holme, at Caswell Bay, about a mile and a half from Newton, knew the answers to the many questions which plagued him.

Shotton — dapper, of medium height, with a shock of frizzy jet-black hair, deep-brown piercing eyes, and a dark face which lit up on occasions with an unusually attractive smile — was all surface charm and co-operation.

Yes, he had known Mamie. Yes, well — *very* well. And yes, (those dark eyes of his downcast in candid shame), they had lived together.

Married her? Oh, no. How could he? He had a wife and a child already, hadn't he? (Frank, disingenuous look.)

When did I last see her? Let me think. It would have been about the 5th or 6th of December — in Oxford Street, Swansea. We'd had a quarrel, you know. Separated. Finished.

Plausible. But the police were not satisfied. They began to dig. Slowly, meticulously, they uncovered the facts of the bitter-sweet romance between the gay, vivacious Mamie, and the dour, suspicious and apparently violent man whom she had "married". From the lips of friends and family and acquaintances, from the mute testimony of letters, the picture of a stormy, jealousy-riven relationship emerged.

Mrs Hearn remembered: "On one occasion Mamie Shotton made a very strange remark to me. She said, 'If I am ever missing, do your very utmost to find me, won't you?' "

There was a letter from Mamie to her parents: "If you don't hear from me, please wire to Mrs Hearn and see if she knows anything about me. The man is not all there. I don't think I will live with him very long. I am very much afraid of him. My life is not worth living." That was in July 1919.

And there were letters from Shotton to the girl he called "Wifie". One, written from the Compton Hotel, Church Street, Liverpool, contained the words, "I gave myself to you long ago, but you never seemed to care after the first few weeks. . . . I gave you my name and my love, and you trifled with both".

He had obviously begun to suspect that his "own little darling" was being unfaithful to him — as indeed she was.

Letter from Mamie to her boy-friend: "My dearest Dalbert — Awfully sorry, old Boy, for not writing you sooner, only you must know how very careful I have got to be. . . . I am leaving Cardiff, I think, tomorrow, so if you wire my fare to Sunderland I will leave straightaway and be with you very shortly, and we will make up for lost time. . . . My old man seems to know quite a lot . . . but what the eyes don't see, the heart can't grieve. . . . Am just dying to see you and feel your dear arms around me."

Convinced now that Shotton was their man, the police

The only known photograph of Everard Shotton and Mamie Stuart together

nevertheless went through the motions of circulating Mamie's description all over Britain: Age 26. Of very attractive appearance. Height 5 ft. 3 in. or 4 in. Well built. Profusion of dark brown hair, worn bobbed. Dark grey eyes. Four faint teeth marks on right cheek, the result of a dog-bite when a child.

But, secretly, they were looking for a corpse.

They searched every last inch of Ty-Llanwydd, and, several times, dug over the garden which surrounded it. They searched and dug much of the adjacent countryside, too.

They found nothing.

Even so, on 29 May 1920, Shotton was arrested — and charged with bigamy.

By now he was admitting that he was the man who had left the portmanteau at the Grosvenor Hotel: "After we had finally parted I went back to Ty-Llanwydd and found a whole lot of her things all screwed up on the floor. I put them in a small attaché-case and took them to my office, and afterwards to the Grosvenor Hotel, and left them there."

He duly appeared at Glamorgan Assizes in July. His defence that it was not him, but someone impersonating him, who had married Mamie at South Shields, failed to impress the jury, and on 27 July he was sentenced to eighteen months' hard labour by Mr Justice Avory.

And that, had it not been for the millionth-chance twist of fate on a November day forty-one years later, would have been the end of the story.

On Sunday, 5 November 1961 — the precise anniversary of the day that Mamie Stuart travelled for the last time from Sunderland to Swansea — three young pot-holers, John Gerke, Graham Jones and Colin MacNamara, were exploring a disused lead-mine sunk into the cliff top at Brandy Cove, on the Gower coast of Glamorgan.

And there, in the dank and darkness of a bat-infested cavern at the base of an old air-shaft, fifty feet underground, they stumbled upon the secret tomb — and the perfect murder. There, they found Mamie Stuart.

The lady had been sawn not in half, but into three. Her skeleton lay hidden behind artfully placed boulders and a three-inch-thick stone slab. Around the bones were swaddled the rotted remains of a sack. Nearby lay a black butterfly comb, a tuft of brown hair still attached to it, and two rings — a broad, gold wedding-ring, and an engagement-ring, set with three stones.

At Cardiff's forensic science laboratory, Home Office pathologist Dr William Reginald James and Dr John Lewis Griffiths reassembled the bones into the skeleton of a woman: age, between twenty-four and twenty-eight; estimated height, 5 foot 3 inches. Transparencies of the skull, projected on to photographs of Mamie taken during her theatrical career, showed indisputable corresponding features between the two.

Most of those who had actually known Mamie were either dead or doddering, but an elderly woman, Elsie Evans, who had been her intimate friend, was able to identify her rings. In all, twenty witnesses told their stories to the coroner and his jury.

The strangest tale of all was that of an eighty-three-year-old retired postman, William Symons.

He said that one afternoon in 1919, he had seen Shotton struggling with a heavy sack outside Ty-Llanwydd. Shotton glanced up and his eye caught a glimpse of the brass buttons on Symons' blue uniform. "Oh, God!" he exclaimed, "For a minute I thought you were a policeman." Symons offered to help carry the sack to Shotton's yellow van, which was standing outside the gate. "No, no, no," said Shotton, who then put the sack in the van and drove off in the direction of Brandy Cove.

It did not take the jury long to reach their verdict: that the skeleton was that of Mamie Stuart, that she was murdered, and that the evidence pointed to George Shotton's being her murderer.

But as it turned out, Shotton was beyond the jurisdiction of that or any other court.

It had taken a three-week, country-wide search, involving Interpol, Scotland Yard and nine police forces, to track him down to Bristol's Southmead Hospital, where, on 30 April 1958, aged seventy-eight and penniless, he had died.

For nearly three years his body had lain in grave No. 000405 in Arno's Vale Cemetery, Bristol.

It is a weed-grown, unmarked grave. No headstone. No inscription. His only epitaph, the words spoken by Mrs Edna Collins, the woman in whose home in Coronation Road, Bristol, he was during his last years a paying guest:

"He was," she said, "such a perfect gentleman."

Mamie Stuart's epitaph was spoken by Mr D. R. James, a poetic Welsh coroner:

"They found her, between highland and lowland, in a coign of a cliff; by a silver sea, without a grave, uncoffined, unknelled and unknown."

But now her pathetic little ghost has risen to attain a kind of immortality as one of the legends in the murder-will-out folklore of crime.

145

W. Lloyd Woodland

The victim in what was generally spoken of as the Southampton Garage Mystery, Mr Vivian Messiter, had only been living in Southampton six weeks. The murderer had only been in Southampton eleven days, while their association could only have existed about five days when the murder was committed and the body of the victim locked in the garage where it lay undiscovered for a period of more than two months.

Mr Vivian Messiter at the time of his death was some fifty-seven or fifty-eight years of age. He came of a well-to-do family in the West country, and was brought up in Somersetshire. As a young man he was active, athletic, and full of the spirit of adventure. He went abroad early in life, and thereafter was in England only on holiday. When the Great War broke out, his adventurous spirit prompted him, as it did so many others overseas, to come to the aid of the Old Country. Despite the fact that he was over forty years of age, and there was no legal obligation upon him to serve, he nevertheless joined up, and served in France until he was shot through both thighs and incapacitated. He made a recovery after some time, but he was permanently lamed in the right leg, being compelled to use a stick for walking.

He seems to have grown a little weary of overseas life, and was anxious to find a congenial occupation in England. Like many adventurous individuals, he had not gathered much wealth, and if he was to settle in England he needed to work. To this end he had secured a post as the agent for the sale of lubricating oils in Hampshire, and, about the middle of September, 1928, he came to Southampton as a suitable centre from which to carry on the work of that agency.

He took lodgings at 3 Carlton Road, where he proved a

most methodical guest. His days were ordered with business-like regularity. He had no friends or visitors of either sex, and his time seemed to be spent almost wholly upon the pursuit of his work.

It would appear that Messiter very soon realized that he was' hampered in his work for want of knowledge of local conditions. This caused him to insert an advertisement in a local paper, toward the end of September, for persons who could supply this lack and act as sub-agents for the sale of the oil.

On the morning of Tuesday, 30 October 1928, Messiter asked to be called early, and to have his breakfast at half-past seven. It was a break from his methodical life, for he had never before asked to be called, and he had never previously had his breakfast earlier than eight o'clock. He left the house about eight o'clock, ostensibly to go to the store at 42 Grove Street, where he kept his oils, and his two-seater Morris Oxford car. From that time he was never again seen alive by anybody at his apartments, nor, so far as is known, by any of his business acquaintances in the town.

At first his disappearance was a mere domestic matter, interesting only his landlord and his employers. Mr Parrot, his landlord, finding he did not return, went round to the store in Grove Street on 1 November to see whether anything was wrong there. He found both outer and inner doors securely locked. It seemed as though Messiter had gone away from Southampton, possibly in his car. Not enough was known about him or his business to make any reasonable guess as to what he had done.

His firm, the Wolf's Head Oil Company, not hearing from him in routine manner, wrote to 42 Grove Street, but received no reply. This was quite natural, as it turned out, because their letters lay untouched in the letter-box on the outer gate of the store. Further inquiries by the firm, through the police, resulted in a policeman being sent round to 42 Grove Street to investigate. He, too, found the outer doors securely locked. Peering through the letter-box, he saw that the inner doors of the store were also securely locked; he returned to the police

Vivian Messiter

station and reported accordingly.

This was the state of things at Christmas, 1928. The Wolf's Head Oil Company were puzzled and annoyed at the sudden and mysterious disappearance of their Hampshire representative just at a time when he had professed to be zealous in working up a connection for them in the district. Mr and Mrs Parrot did not know what to think. It seemed possible that Messiter had become disgusted with the prospects of his agency, had dropped the whole thing like a hot potato, and had gone elsewhere. But somehow their previous short experience of Messiter, who was nothing if not courteous, gave them a feeling that he was not the sort of man to treat his host and hostess in so scurvy a fashion. So, having an address in New York to which Messiter had written, they at length wrote there saying what had happened.

As far as the oil company was concerned, nothing was done

until the New Year. Then a new agent was appointed, Mr Passmore. This young man, in company with a friend, went round to 42 Grove Street, to take over the store and garage about eleven o'clock on the morning of Thursday, 10 January 1929. Mr Passmore had to gain access to the forecourt of the premises by climbing over a wall which divided the place from a public house. Having got into the forecourt, he found that the doors of the store were padlocked, and he had to get the assistance of a workman employed at the public house to force the padlock. Having got the door open, Mr Passmore and his friend entered the place, a long narrow store, 44 feet in length by 12 feet 6 inches wide. Immediately inside the door they found a red two-seater Morris Oxford car, loaded with five cases of oil, as if ready for a journey, or just returned from one. Passmore tried to start the car, but without avail. There was no petrol in the tank, and the car apparently had not been run for weeks.

Leaving the car, Passmore and his friend began to explore the store, noting the cases and drums of oil stacked around the walls, and some of the cases at the far end ranged in a tier like a partition wall. Behind this tier, out of sight from the doorway, they found the body of a man, the exposed face of which showed a ghastly injury to the left eye. The mystery of the whereabouts of Mr Messiter was solved. The condition of the body left no doubt that it must have lain there for many weeks. Where the left eye had been was a great hole. At first it seemed as though the unfortunate man had been shot at close quarters by a weapon carrying an expanding bullet of a large calibre. Blood was spattered on several of the adjacent oil cases, and on one which lay beside the body was a patch of blood six inches or so across. No weapon was visible, either in the dead man's hand or upon the floor. It was obviously a case of murder. Suicide was out of the question, for, although a man may shoot himself through the left eye, he cannot thereafter lock himself in and spirit away the weapon.

The police were called, and, after careful note had been taken of the position of the body and its surroundings, it was removed to the borough mortuary where, later, exhaustive pathological examinations were made by Dr Seager Thomas, Senior Police Surgeon of Southampton, and Sir Bernard Spilsbury, Honorary Pathologist to the Home Office. Before they had completed their examinations, the police pursued a rigorous search for a bullet or bullets which they imagined must have passed through the skull.

But the pathologists soon discovered that the murder had been perpetrated not by a firearm, but by some blunt instrument such as a hammer or a spanner. The murderer had delivered three terrific blows, each of which had crushed the skull like an eggshell. After exhaustive examination, both doctors agreed as to the manner in which the crime had been committed. The victim had been bending forward at the instant that the first blow was struck on the nape of the neck, crushing the skull at a point just above where it joined the backbone, and having the effect of pole-axing. The stunned and dying man must have dropped like a stone, with the left side of his head falling on the oil case where was found the large patch of blood. While in this position, with the right ear uppermost, a second blow was struck just above and in front of the ear, this blow cracking the inner floor of the skull from side to side. The reflex action in the insensible body must then have caused a stiffening and a contraction of the limbs so that the body rolled off the case on to its back. The murderer then delivered his third and last blow on the left eyebrow, the weapon crashing through the frontal bones to the brain beneath.

Any one of these blows was sufficient to cause death almost immediately. Nor would such blows be likely to cause a spurting of blood upon the clothes or person of the murderer. It was conjectured at first that the murderer had struck Mr Messiter down in some other part of the garage, afterwards dragging the body into the recess where it was found; but there was no evidence of this. It is practically certain that he waited, with cold cunning, until his victim was working unsuspectingly behind the tier of cases, and, stealing up behind him, struck him down.

The deed done, there was no need to touch the body to place

Exterior of Garage

it in partial concealment. It had already fallen in the most suitable place for the murderer's wishes. All he needed to do now was to search the clothing for money and valuables. Next he must have searched the garage for any documents which might link him with the dead man, removing some leaves from two of Mr Messiter's books which were in his car. But he failed to see two very important scraps of paper, one on the floor, black with dirt and grease, and the other screwed up into a ball and thrown into a rubbish box at the end of the store. He then locked up the premises.

The Chief Constable of Southampton, realizing that it was a case of unusual difficulty, and one which possibly involved much more than local inquiry, wisely decided to ask for the assistance of Scotland Yard. Chief Inspector Prothero, one of the ablest men in the CID, was sent down, with Detective Inspector Young as his assistant. They received unstinted help from Detective Inspector Chatfield of the Southampton police force, his local knowledge being of great assistance in appraising the worth of the local clues. These three, with their subordinates, succeeded in a very short space of time in solving the mystery of the murderer of Mr Messiter.

At first sight the mystery of the murderer appeared impenetrable. Very few people knew anything about Mr Messiter, much less about his associates, or employees, if he had any. A grocer recalled that about the time of his disappearance he had been seen in the company of a young man of about 5 feet 4 inches in height, with a blue suit, and of brisk appearance. Apart from a distant relative whom he had visited on the Sunday before his disappearance, at Sarisbury, a village some eight miles to the south-east of Southampton, and his dentist, with whom he was to have dined on the evening of the very day he disappeared, nobody could be found who had had any definite association with him outside of his lodgings.

Was the crime the result of a vendetta begun somewhere overseas? Was it the work of a marauder surprised in attempted depredation? Was it the result of a quarrel with an associate? Or again, was it the hand of a homicidal maniac which had struck Messiter down with so unerring an aim? These, and others, were the kind of questions which confronted Mr Prothero and his assistants.

The first clue that came to hand was found in a memorandum book which, with a duplicate order book, was on the driving seat of Messiter's car. Beside the books were found also Messiter's wash-leather driving gloves, and a pocket electric torch. The clue in the memorandum book was a receipt for half a crown paid as commission for the sale of oil. It was signed by "H. F. Galton", and it was dated 30 October 1928, the very day upon which Messiter disappeared. Strangely enough, it was the only receipt in the book; at least, the only one visible to the casual eye.

H. F. Galton was soon found. He proved to be an employee of the Southern Railway, and he at once admitted having been paid half a crown commission by Messiter. He, however, declared he had been paid this sum at his own house, where Messiter had come in his car with the oil which Galton was to pass on to the customer he had secured, and in respect of the

153

sale of which the half-crown had been paid as commission. He said he had never seen Messiter elsewhere than at his, Galton's, house, and in fact he did not know where Messiter's store was situated. Moreover, after thinking back to the time of the sale of the oil, Galton was positive the commission was paid, and the receipt was given, on 29 October, the Monday evening, and not the Tuesday when the receipt was dated. He explained that Messiter gave him an invoice dated 30 October because he was to deliver the oil to the customer on the 30th, and the receipt for the commission was given the same date. It was proved independently that Galton had been at work at Redbridge from the early morning of 30 October until about five o'clock the same day. As the police were satisfied that Mr Messiter must have been murdered during the day of 30 October, and most probably in the morning, it was clear that Galton, despite the obvious "pointer" in the memorandum book, could have had nothing to do with the crime.

The police scrutinized the two books found on the driving seat of the car more closely. They noticed two facts of importance. One was that from each book leaves had been removed, and the other was that upon one of the leaves in the memorandum book there were impressions, or indentations, made by a pencil which had been used upon a missing leaf. These indicated a receipt for commission, similar to that of Galton's, but signed by "W. F. T.", and dated apparently 28 October 1928. At once the questions arose, who was W. F. T., and why should his receipt have been removed from the book, while Galton's was left?

It was also noticed that in the duplicate order book were a couple of carbon sheets. They had evidently been used by Messiter for duplicating orders, and, also, what proved to be far more important, for duplicating receipts for money paid for commission on sales of oil. The names and addresses disclosed by scrutiny of these carbon sheets gave the police a great deal of trouble. Every one of them proved to be bogus both in name and place.

The details of the receipt shown by the indentations in the memorandum book also appeared in one of the carbon sheets.

It was, "Received from Wolf's Head Oil Company commission on Cromers & Bartlett, 5 gall. at 5s. 6d., commission 2s.6d.", accompanied by the date and the initials W. F. T. On one of the carbon sheets "Cromer & Bartlett, 25 Bold Street, Southampton" appeared. Other names were "Jervis, The Crescent, Bassett, Southampton", and "Baskerfield, Clayton Farm, Bentley Road, near Winchester". All were bogus names and addresses. What could have been taking place in Messiter's business affairs in the days immediately before he disappeared? Why should he be making entries in his order book concerning firms which did not exist at places which could not be found?

The only conclusion a reasonable person could come to was that somebody had been handing in bogus orders, and, considering the receipt shown by the indentations, he had been collecting commission upon those same bogus orders. Who was this individual, and where was he? What had been his relations with Messiter?

The police, naturally, did not stop there. A minute search of the garage was made which brought to light two pieces of paper. One was a torn scrap bearing some writing, but so soiled with dirt and oil as to be almost indecipherable. The other was a crumpled ball of paper which when opened out proved to be a note written by Messiter in these terms: "Mr W. F. Thomas. I shall be at 42 Grove Street at 10 a.m. but not at noon. V. Messiter." "W. F. Thomas" corresponded with the initials W. F. T. below the indentation receipt for commission in the memorandum book. And when the torn and dirty scrap of paper had been scientifically cleaned of the oil and dirt, the same name, W. F. Thomas, was found to be upon it.

One other thing was found in the garage during the search. This was a large hammer of unusual weight and type. It was found behind the oil drums which were stacked against the wall of the garage, having been dropped down the recess between two piles of drums. It proved to be a French hammer, about 2 lb in weight, square-faced, and wedge-shaped in the rear. It was blood-stained, and upon it were found two hairs of eyebrow-type. These hairs matched exactly two hairs taken

155

from the right eyebrow of the corpse. Clearly this was the weapon with which the murder had been committed. It was found, later, that this hammer belonged to a motor mechanic named Marsh who had bought it in France. Somewhere about the morning of 30 October 1928, or perhaps the day before, someone, having the appearance of a motor mechanic, had called at the garage where Marsh worked in Southampton, about a mile from 42 Grove Street, and had borrowed the hammer.

Meanwhile, the police had visited Mr Messiter's room at 3 Carlton Road, where they found some business books and letters. One of these letters was significant. It had obviously been sent in answer to an advertisement by Messiter for an assistant to sell oil on commission. It ran thus:

W. F. Thomas,
5 Cranberry Avenue, Southampton
23 October 1928
Sir,
Re your advert. of the present inst. Being in the motor trade, and having a good connexion among farmers and garage proprietors, I am sure I can do you good service in the oil lines. I am constantly asked my opinion of such, and I am sure I can build up a good connexion of same.
Trusting I shall have reply to the favour of such.
I am, sir,
Yours truly,
WILLIAM F. THOMAS.

So W. F. Thomas of the scraps of paper in the garage was not a customer of Messiter, but very possibly an employee for the short space of time between the date of the letter and Messiter's disappearance on 30 October. Naturally the police were now anxious to know who and where W. F. Thomas was. They soon found out that others also were wanting to know about him. The Wiltshire police were wanting to know the whereabouts of a motor mechanic giving the name of W. F. Thomas, who had been working for a Mr Mitchell at Downton, near Salisbury, and who was suspected of having stolen a number of wage packets, containing the sum of £143, belonging to Mr Mitchell, a few days before Christmas, 1928.

Immediately, Chief Inspector Prothero took up this clue at Downton. He found that not only had the W. F. Thomas who was wanted by the Wiltshire police gone to Downton from Southampton, but that he had gone there immediately after Messiter had disappeared. Moreover, Mr Mitchell produced a letter which he had received from W. F. Thomas which made it almost certain that the writer was the same individual who had answered Messiter's advertisement. Mr Mitchell had advertised for a motor mechanic, and this was the reply he received:

W. F. Thomas,
5 Cranberry Avenue, Southampton
23 October 1928

Sir,
Re your advert. of the present inst. I shall be pleased to let you have fuller details of my past experience in the motor trade.

I have been in the trade now 15 years and am fully conversant with all the leading makes of cars. I am a married man, no children.

I am willing to undergo any trial you wish, and am not afraid of work, or the number of hours.

I shall be pleased if I may put myself at your disposal. Trusting I shall be able to do so.
I am, sir
Yours truly,
WILLIAM F. THOMAS.

It seems that Mr Mitchell was attracted by this reply to his advertisement, and he sent to the writer offering to meet him Below Bar, Southampton, on Saturday, 27 October, at five o'clock in the afternoon. The appointment was kept, and as a result W. F. Thomas was engaged by Mr Mitchell as a motor mechanic, to start work at Downton on Monday, 5 November. No reference had been asked for by Mr Mitchell, because Thomas had hinted that he was leaving his present employers as he had had "a bit of a noise" with the son of the proprietor.

In the following week the actions of Thomas were more than a little remarkable. Although he was not expecting his new mechanic to begin work until 5 November, to Mr Mitchell's surprise Thomas turned up at Downton in the early afternoon of Tuesday, 30 October, and offered to start work at once. Mr Mitchell told him he could not do that. For one thing he had not given his present mechanic notice, and for another he had made no arrangements for rooms for Thomas, a very necessary matter in a country place like Downton. But Mr Mitchell, with some generosity, agreed to pay him from that day, and repeated that he would be ready for Thomas to start work on the following Monday.

With that, Thomas departed. He had come in some car, but what make it was Mr Mitchell did not know.

It might have been supposed that Thomas, having been promised wages although he was not working that week, would have been content to remain in Southampton until the end of the week; not so. On the Friday morning Mr Mitchell received a letter from him saying he was travelling to Downton that day, ready to take up his work. Mr Mitchell, still having no accommodation for him, sent a telegram telling him not to come, and intimating that a letter would follow.

Notwithstanding this putting off, Thomas appeared to be resolved to get away from Southampton. On the Saturday morning, without waiting for the arrival of Mr Mitchell's letter, Thomas telephoned to Mr Mitchell asking if he might come to Downton that day. Mr Mitchell gave assent and Thomas arrived at Downton about midday on Saturday, 3 November, in company with a fair-haired young woman presumed to be his wife. He was penniless, and had to borrow from Mr Mitchell's clerk in order to pay the fare of the taxicab in which the pair had come from Salisbury. His story was that he had lost his wallet and money on the journey from Southampton.

Thomas worked for Mr Mitchell until the third week in December. About the 21st there occurred a mysterious theft of wage packets from Mr Mitchell's counting house. Thomas was closely questioned by the Wiltshire police concerning this theft. Among other things, they wanted to know the name and address of the firm for which he had worked at Southampton. His reply, taken in conjunction with the markings in the memorandum book and carbon sheets found on the driving seat of Messiter's car, was significant. It was "Allied Transports, Bold Street, Southampton".

While the Wiltshire police were making inquiries into this address at Southampton, Thomas disappeared, so precipitately that he did not trouble about belongings at his lodgings. He and the blonde woman vanished from Downton, and, so far as the Wiltshire police were concerned, all trace of them was lost.

Chief Inspector Prothero decided that the most rigorous search must be made for this W. F. Thomas. He was not sure then whether the name was real or assumed. But a careful search of Thomas's lodgings at Downton brought to light a scrap of paper, thrown away behind a stove, on which were the words "Podmore" and "Manchester".

Manchester police were at once communicated with, and they replied that a young motor mechanic named William Henry Podmore was wanted in their jurisdiction for fraudulent conversion of the proceeds of the sale of motor vehicles. Now the question arose: Were William Henry Podmore and William F. Thomas one and the same person?

Further inquiries had meanwhile been pursued in Southampton, particularly at 5 Cranberry Avenue, where W. F. Thomas and the fair-haired woman who was supposed to be his wife, had lodged. It was found that they had arrived there on Saturday, 20 October 1928, and Thomas had paid fifteen shillings in advance, a week's rent for a bed sitting-room. According to Mrs Horne, the landlady, and her son, Thomas appeared to be a motor mechanic, but he never told them where he was working. He hinted that he had been sent down from London by his firm to work in Southampton. At the end of the first week Thomas did not pay his next week's rent, although Mrs Horne was herself in need of it; but he paid her the fifteen shillings about six o'clock on the evening of Tuesday, 30 October, the day Messiter disappeared.

When Thomas paid Mrs Horne on the Tuesday he had told

her he would be leaving Southampton that week, saying he was "going back to the head office in London". On the Friday he said he was expecting a letter. This letter had not come when he left about nine o'clock on the Saturday morning, and he gave an address to which the letter might be forwarded. The address, "29R Chiswick Road", was fictitious.

Chief Inspector Prothero decided to publish a full description of W. F. Thomas and the woman who had been with him. His height, build, and colour of hair and eyes were easily ascertained, for a number of people had seen him at Downton, and had worked with him for weeks. In particular, he bore a definite scar on his face. Accordingly, on the night of 15 January, the description of the pair was issued to the press and the provincial police.

Immediately, the Stoke-on-Trent police were struck with the similarity of the description of Thomas to William Henry Podmore, a man whom they knew only too well as an incorrigible offender, a daring and plausible thief. They knew he had been associating with a fair-haired girl named Lily Hambleton, of Sneyd Green, Hanley, and the phrase "Golden-haired Lil" appearing in the official description, confirmed them in their suspicion. They began to look for both Podmore and the girl Lily Hambleton.

They were too late to see Podmore. He had paid a flying visit to the Potteries, but had gone as swiftly as he had come. They were more fortunate in their search for Lily Hambleton, for they found her at her home. She had just arrived, having parted from Podmore only a few hours before. This was on 17 January, exactly one week after the discovery of Messiter's dead body in the Southampton garage. The Hanley police questioned Lily Hambleton as to Podmore's whereabouts. She declared that he had gone to Southampton, via London, to be interviewed by the police concerning the death of Messiter. They had seen the police appeal for W. F. Thomas to come forward, and they had decided that he must go to Southampton.

The next question was: At what hotel or boarding house in London had Podmore stopped before? Miss Hambleton said

William Henry Podmore

they had stayed at the Leicester Hotel in Vauxhall Bridge Road when going to Southampton in the middle of October, and had stayed there at Christmas time when coming from Downton. This information was at once passed to New Scotland Yard, and in the early hours of the following morning Podmore was found at the Leicester Hotel. When he was addressed by the officers who had come for him, he said, "I know what you want me for, but I can explain everything of my movements at Southampton."

Whether in very fact he was on his way to Southampton, or whether he had fled to London as a safer place than the Midlands in which to hide, is a matter which can only be guessed at. He had registered at the Leicester Hotel in the name of Podmore, but no doubt by that time he was more than eager to drop the name of W. F. Thomas. When the police appeared, he made a virtue of necessity, and professed himself ready to go to Southampton for examination. He also declared

161

that he had tried to telephone to New Scotland Yard when he arrived in London the night before, but was told the "line was out of order".

When Podmore was taken to Southampton, the psychology of the man emerged. An egoist of an exaggerated type, he was cock-sure that he could tell such a tale to the police as would satisfy them that he was innocent of the death of Mr Messiter. He had some reason for his confidence. Several times in his career he had brought off profitable coups by very ingenious fictions. And not only was he, as Lord Hewart said at the trial, "a ready and ingenious inventor of what is not true," but he had what is often missing from the make-up of prevaricators, a most excellent memory. He knew he was not likely to make the crude mistakes so often made by those who essay to build a story to meet a desperate situation.

So, when he came face to face with Chief Inspector Prothero and Detective Sergeant Young, he was quietly confident that he could satisfy them that, although he might be guilty of offences at Manchester, he knew nothing about Messiter's death. But, because he did not know how much the police knew, he made some crucial admissions, the most important being that he had been with Messiter in the garage at Grove Street on the morning of 30 October, the day of the murder. This admission was the very keystone of the case which was built up against him. When he admitted that he was on the premises at 42 Grove Street from 9.30 until noon on the fatal day, he did not then know that he was admitting that he was the last man to see Messiter alive, so far as could be ascertained. It is certain that, had he known what the police knew when he began his statement, he would have denied being near the garage at all on 30 October. His statement was voluminous, full of much petty detail. He built up a plausible story in which a vast amount of unimportant truth was interwoven with some judicious fiction. Having admitted that he was in the garage with Messiter on the morning of 30 October, he had to make some allegation which would clear himself of complicity in the murder.

It will be remembered that Galton's receipt for commission

had been left in the memorandum book found in the car in the garage. Whoever had removed the receipt signed W. F. T. had thought it worth while to leave Galton's receipt in the book for anyone to see. Podmore said that when he first went to Messiter's garage Messiter was there with another man whom he introduced as Maxton or Baxton. He went on: "I am almost sure the agent's name was Mr Maxton or Mr Baxton. . . . On Monday I reported, as asked, at half-past nine. Mr Messiter and the agent were there when I arrived. They were talking about an order sold, and I saw money pass from Mr Messiter to the agent, which I heard mentioned as half a crown. Mr Messister put an entry, and asked the agent to sign. The agent did sign. I took it to be a receipt for the commission paid to him for the sale of five gallons of oil. . . . On Monday I only stayed about half an hour, and I left the agent and Mr Messiter together. . . . On Tuesday morning, 30 October, I went to the garage between 9 and 9.30. . . . The agent and Mr Messiter were there. They were having trouble with the magneto. Mr Messiter asked me if I could see to it and any other minor job, after which he left me. The agent left with him."

There was not a tittle of evidence, save Podmore's statement, that there ever was another man besides himself assisting Messiter in those last days of October. When he was making his statement, Podmore was unaware that the police had seen Galton, and had satisfied themselves that Galton had absolutely nothing to do with the murder, or, indeed, with Mr Messiter, save two meetings at Galton's own house.

Podmore was now in custody, and, as there were outstanding charges against him for offences prior to the murder of Messiter, there was no need to be precipitate in advancing the charge of murder, even though the police felt convinced he was indeed the murderer. Suspicion, however strong, would not be sufficient to secure a conviction. Much remained to be done. There was the incident of the borrowed hammer to be cleared up, if possible. There was more to be looked into in the matter of the supposed bogus orders which had, seemingly, been given to Messiter; and Podmore's doings on and after 30 October needed to be investigated.

It was found that immediately after Christmas, 1928, which Podmore and Miss Hambleton spent at the Leicester Hotel in London, they went to Birmingham. When there, Podmore answered an advertisement for a joint post at the Stonebridge Hotel, Merriden, Warwickshire, a man to look after the garage and a woman to work as indoor servant, wages £2 per week together, and all found. The proprietor of the Stonebridge Hotel engaged them, and Podmore and Miss Hambleton began to work at the hotel on 5 January. On the following Friday the newspapers were full of the story of the discovery of Messiter's body in the garage at Southampton. About noon the next day, Saturday, Podmore asked for his week's money, saying they were leaving. He was told they would be paid when the stock in the garage had been taken. But he would not wait for this. He and Miss Hambleton left the hotel, travelling back to Birmingham by motor-bus, without their wages.

Podmore's explanation of this curious behaviour was that the hours of service at that hotel were too long for him to put up with any longer, and he preferred to leave without wages. He left when he did because he "wanted to catch the bus to Birmingham". "How often do the buses run from Merriden to Birmingham?" asked the Lord Chief Justice, when Podmore was giving evidence upon this point. "Every half-hour," was Podmore's reply. "Then you could have caught another bus in half an hour?" queried his lordship. "Yes," said Podmore.

The prosecution suggested that Podmore's strange action at Merriden was occasioned because he was alarmed by the news of the finding of the body of Messiter, and his instinct was to bury himself in a crowded city where he would be less conspicuous. He had no reason at that time to fear that the police would know anything about "W. F. Thomas" of Southampton and Downton, much less connect "W. F. Thomas" with William Henry Podmore. But it may be suspected that he judged he would be safer away from any garage or motor employment. If he was alarmed on Friday the 11th, so that he left without his wages on Saturday the 12th, he must have been in a far worse state of mind on the following

Thursday, when the press of the whole country was inquiring for W. F. Thomas, the "man with the scar". He knew no place in the Midlands where he could lie hidden. What better hiding-place than London?

On the request of New Scotland Yard, the Stoke-on-Trent police made some inquiries concerning the names and addresses in Mr Messiter's two books and on the carbon sheets in one of them. They were able to say at once that although there might be none in Southampton or in Hampshire, there were three or four Bold Streets in the region of the Potteries. It will be remembered that not only did Bold Street appear in Messiter's books and on the carbon sheets, but Podmore himself used the name at Downton, giving it to the police there as the Southampton address of the firm for whom he said he had worked.

Another of the names appearing in Messiter's books, on the carbon sheets, was that of Jervis, while another was Ben Baskerfield, Clayton Farm, Bentley Road, near Winchester. It was discovered that "Jervis" and "Clayton Farm" were names in close proximity to Podmore's home. A milkman supplying milk next door to Podmore's home occupied a Clayton farm, and another farming family within a mile of his home bore the name of Jervis.

The association with the name Baskerfield is a little more curious. In 1919 Podmore was in the hands of the police, and the police sergeant who arrested him was named Baskeyfield. But Podmore, apparently not knowing how the name was spelt, and mistaking the pronunciation, repeatedly referred to the sergeant as Baskerfield. The prosecution suggested to the jury that the appearance of the names Baskerfield, and Clayton Farm, and Jervis, and Bold Street, in the entries in Mr Messiter's books and on the carbon sheets, were not mere accidental coincidences, but were proof that Podmore, in whose mind were all these names, had used them in giving bogus orders to Messiter for the purpose of collecting commission fraudulently.

The crime may now be reconstructed. Finding Mr Messiter an

easy-going individual who was ready to pay out commission before he received the money for the orders handed in, Podmore began to defraud him from the outset of their association. Following the lines of his letter, which boasted a "good connexion among farmers and garage proprietors", Podmore handed to Mr Messiter several bogus orders, one at least bearing the address of a farm, while "Cromer & Bartlett, Bold Street, Southampton" may have been put forward as a firm of garage proprietors. Podmore knew well that these frauds would not remain long undiscovered. But, on the heels of his engagement with Messiter, he had secured another post at a distance from Southampton, and was contemplating taking up that appointment within a day or two.

He was desperately in need of money, not merely to pay his week's rent, but to supply his own and Miss Hambleton's day-to-day needs. He had previously obtained money by theft or fraud a number of times. He was now in as desperate a case for cash as he had ever been. Did he resolve upon murder, calculating that Messiter would be carrying upon him several pounds which, with his watch and any other valuables, could be taken and converted into cash? He may even have considered the possibility of stealing Mr Messiter's car and selling it. Indeed, there is evidence that he drove Miss Hambleton and himself in that car to Downton on the afternoon of 30 October, the occasion when he visited Mr Mitchell and offered to begin work at once. But he saw, after reflection, that it would be too dangerous to steal and sell the car. In the same way he came to the conclusion that it was too risky to attempt to dispose of Messiter's watch and chain. So he dropped them, with Messiter's keys, in the lavatory cistern of a public convenience in Southampton, where they were not discovered for many months.

At the trial, the judge in his summing-up said it was stretching human credulity too far to suggest that after murdering Mr Messiter on the morning of 30 October, Podmore then drove Messiter's car to Downton, brought it back, and then placed it inside the garage where lay the stiffened body of his victim. But, bearing in mind the extraordinary egoism of Podmore, and the story which he later told of taking the car out to try it, after he had spent some two hours repairing it, a story he had probably prepared before or at the time of the murder, the suggestion is not so impossible as it appears at first sight. It was a daring move, designed to serve more than one purpose. It enabled him to see Mr Mitchell, but more than that, it was designed to provide a plausible alibi. If he returned to the garage and found the murder discovered, his instant answer would have been: "This must have happened while I was away. I left Mr Messiter hale and well when I went out at his bidding to try his car for him." There would have been the French hammer, behind the oil drums, to point to some stranger as the assailant.

This French hammer, which had been borrowed from the motor mechanic Marsh, either on the morning of the murder or the day before, suggests proof that the murder was planned.

Except for the sinister purpose for which it was used, there was no known reason for Podmore, or anyone else working at 42 Grove Street, to borrow a hammer, much less a hammer of such a weight. After the murder had been discovered, there was found in the tool kit of the car at the garage a hammer of the normal size supplied by the makers for repair work on the car. There was also a case opener in the garage for opening the cases and crates. For what conceivable purpose could a 2 lb hammer be required by anybody in the garage?

The conclusion can hardly be resisted that Podmore, having deliberately planned to murder Mr Messiter, casting about in his mind what weapon to use to carry out his purpose, conceived the idea of borrowing a heavy hammer "for a job on a car", knowing by experience the readiness of mechanics to help a fellow-worker in this way.

The murder once planned, and the weapon near to the murderer's hand, the rest was easy. The victim was struck down from behind while working in the very spot the murderer had planned he should fall. It has been thought by some that the murder was the culmination of a quarrel between murderer and victim over the bogus orders, but the significant presence of the borrowed hammer in the garage is a factor which appears to negative this theory and to prove premeditation.

Another feature of the case must now be referred to. That is the long delay which ensued between the first arrest of Podmore, and his being charged with murder.

In January 1929, when Podmore was first arrested, the police had not completed their case in respect of the murder charge. Podmore was therefore taken to Manchester and there tried for the two offences outstanding against him of the fraudulent conversion of money for the sale of a motor-car and a motor-cycle. He received two consecutive sentences of three months, and served them.

By the end of March the case against Podmore for the murder of Mr Messiter was complete and was laid before the law officers of the Crown. Just at this time a General Election was imminent. The decision to launch the prosecution was not made when the General Election took place. There was a change in government and consequently a change in the law officers. The new Attorney-General had to fight his seat a second time.

The time for the release of Podmore came, and still no decision had been reached concerning the murder charge. The Wiltshire police took action in respect of the theft of the £143 at Downton. Podmore was arrested at the prison gates on release, and charged at Salisbury with the Downton offence. On the plea of local prejudice, he got the case transferred to the Old Bailey. There he pleaded guilty, receiving a sentence of six months, which he served at Wandsworth. By this time the murder charge was being considered afresh, but the long vacation intervened. Upon his release from Wandsworth in December 1929, he was rearrested, charged with murder, and brought before the magistrates at Southampton. Among witnesses for the prosecution were four prisoners, each of whom said that Podmore, while in prison, had made statements to them concerning the murder. At the end of the proceedings it was only by a majority decision of the magistrates that Podmore was committed for trial.

The trial was opened before the Lord Chief Justice, Lord Hewart of Bury, at the Hampshire Winter Assizes, at the Castle of Winchester, on Monday, 3 March 1930. Sir Thomas Inskip, KC, formerly Attorney-General, appeared for the Crown, with Mr J. G. Trapnell; and the prisoner was defended by Mr H. du Parcq, KC, and Mr T. R. C. Goff. The trial lasted throughout the week before a jury composed wholly of men. The conclusion was reached about three o'clock on the Saturday afternoon. Podmore was found guilty, and sentenced to death.

It was decided at once by Podmore's advisers to take the case to the Court of Criminal Appeal. The main ground of appeal was that the admission of the documents found in the car in the garage was in defiance of an old rule of English law which forbade the writing of a deceased person being given in evidence unless it could be proved that the writing had been made in pursuance of a duty to his employers, or was against his own interest to make. Mr du Parcq, at the outset of the case, had raised this point, urging that these documents, found upon the driving seat of Messiter's car, were inadmissible under this old rule. Sir Thomas Inskip contended that they were admissible because they formed part of the surrounding circumstances of the case, and therefore the jury were entitled to see them in order to draw from them what inferences they thought fit in relation to the guilt or innocence of the accused. Lord Hewart admitted them.

The point was argued before the Court of Criminal Appeal at great length by Mr du Parcq. Many precedents were quoted, but all of them related to civil causes. Not a single precedent relating to a murder was quoted. Sir Thomas Inskip made the same submission as he had done before Lord Hewart, saying that, although he was sure he could prove that the entries had been made in the course of Mr Messiter's duty to his employers and so would be admissible under the old rule, he nevertheless preferred to take the ground that the documents formed part of the surrounding circumstances of the case and were therefore admissible.

The court, Mr Justice Avory presiding, with Justices

Branson and Finlay, ruled that the decision of the Lord Chief Justice was correct and that the documents had been properly admitted. Indeed, the decision seems in accordance with common sense, because supposing the documents had been found clutched in the hand of the dead man, how could it be expected that they could have been kept out of sight of the jury? What logical difference is there between being found on the body, and found close to it? Anything found near the body of a murdered person may be most cogent evidence to determine who committed the crime.

As for the secondary ground of appeal, that the summing-up had omitted certain features of Podmore's defence, Mr Justice Avory observed that it was the usual ground put forward in murder cases. The judges of the appeal were unable to find any misdirection, or any omission which would amount to a misdirection, capable of misleading the jury. On the contrary, they considered the summing-up was a most elaborate review of all the evidence, coupled with repeated warnings to the jury not to convict unless they were without any reasonable doubt of the guilt of the accused. The appeal would therefore be dismissed.

After the dismissal of the appeal, the very unusual course was taken of requesting the Attorney-General to give his sanction under the provisions of the Criminal Appeal Act, 1907, to an appeal to the House of Lords on the point of law raised by the defence in the matter of the documents found in the garage. The Attorney-General, after considering the case, refused to give his sanction.

Meanwhile, a strong movement had been put on foot by some leaders in the Labour world for a petition for a reprieve. Many Labour organizations took the matter up as if it were a political issue. The Independent Labour Party at Birmingham, when the Home Secretary refused to recommend a reprieve, passed a strongly worded resolution condemning this refusal. Mr J. R. Clyne's reply is worthy of record:

> That resolution requires me to ignore the solemn decisions of courts, judges, and jury, and to act upon an opinion of capital

punishment. I hope that no Secretary of State will ever be influenced by such an indefensible doctrine.

In the case in question, I searched for many days in the hope that I would find a reason for recommending a reprieve. I searched in vain. I am not prepared to make a mock of the law, however strong the desire may be to change it. Public opinion of such matters cannot always be guided by the fullest information, and public opinion must not take the place of a court of law. It is the right of the public to change the law. It is the duty of the Minister to apply the law.

The law took its course, Podmore being executed at Winchester Prison on 22 April 1930.

The First Trunk Murder

Jonathan Goodman

It was not until the long hot summer of 1934, when Brighton played host to two trunk-crimes,[1] independent of each other apart from the mutual employment of luggage, that the south-coast resort gained the nickname of Torso City. However, the place was not just doubly deserving of that name, but trebly so — though, admittedly, none of the 1934 Brightonians involved in, or merely intrigued by, the concurrent sensations was anywhere near old enough to have first-hand knowledge of an earlier trunk murder: so far as is known, the inaugurator of the genre in the British Isles.

It happened in 1831. The pioneering murderer was John Holloway, a twenty-six-year-old labourer on the Brighton Chain Pier. Brought up strictly as a Nonconformist, he had dabbled in crime since his teens and was an industrious lecher, possessed of what he termed "a kind of natural love, or it may be called a lustful desire, which some men have towards every woman they look on".

The victim was his estranged wife Celia, whom he had felt constrained to marry in 1825 as a consequence of having made her pregnant. One can understand that the advertised morality of the time left him little alternative — but, even allowing for his indiscriminate lewdness, it is hard to explain why he put himself at risk in the first place. Consider this contemporary description of Celia:

> She was only four feet three inches, being in reality almost a dwarf, so that when either washing or ironing, she was obliged to be placed on a high stool before she could perform her work. Her head was of an extraordinary size in proportion to the rest of her

[1] "A Coincidence of Corpses", *The Railway Murders*, Allison & Busby, 1984.

173

body, and her hands turned outwards, like the paws of a mole. Her features had not the slightest pretension to anything allied to beauty, and on the whole she was rather a repellent object.

It appears that, his distress at Celia's appearance apart, Holloway had more than one motive for killing her.

First, there was the question of money. He had been ordered by the Brighton magistrates to pay his "deserted wife" two shillings a week. This was easier said than done, as he was keeping a woman called Ann Kennett, whom he had bigamously wed, and his weekly take-home pay from the chain pier rarely exceeded three shillings and sixpence. Both women were seven months pregnant, and Holloway feared that, additional to the impending expense of Ann Kennett's baby, he would be ordered to increase the payments to Celia — despite the fact that, as he claimed, he was "not responsible for her sick condition".

There was also a motive of revenge — not only on Celia but on her kin, whom he blamed for most of his misfortunes.

Another motive was jealousy. Like many philanderers, he felt that his own "mere jokes", as he called his dalliances, were no excuse for his wife "to invite other men to shake her bed". In his printed confession, he told of an occasion when he visited Celia late at night:

> She had come down without a candle. She had nothing on but her nightgown, and the landlord came down nearly naked. I could not help noticing that he made as free with Celia in her nightclothes as if he had been her husband, and the more free he made himself, the more pleased she appeared to be. I walked away, to tell the truth, in a great rage.

In July 1831, Holloway rented a house in North Steyne Row for the sole purpose of doing away with Celia. "I went and told her to keep herself in readiness, for in a few days I should come for her to go and live with me. She appeared much delighted at the news." Perhaps to justify the expense, before carrying out the murder-plan Holloway took "a nurse-maid that frequented the pier" to the house and attempted to seduce her —

A correct likeness, from a Painting executed by Mr J. Pares, of Brighton, at the particular request of Mrs Holloway, his Mother, in Horsham Jail

John William Holloway

☞ THIS IS THE ONLY LIKENESS THAT WILL BE ALLOWED TO BE TAKEN

"but when we were there and I took a little too much liberty, she showed symptoms of alarm, which caused me to desist".

After moving Celia's few paltry belongings to the house,

I desired Ann Kennet to be on hand. To that she agreed. But the next thing to be thought of was where was the best place for her to be when I returned. I at last proposed for her to get into the cupboard under the stairs, so that she might be ready in case I should need her assistance.

The plan being thus laid, I went away for Celia, and got some beer on the road. When I got to her lodgings, I found her quite ready; and for dinner she had got a kind of batter-pudding baked. I ate some, but not with a good appetite.

I had made up my mind how I intended to murder her; I was

175

ANN KENNETT.
As she appeared at the Trial of Holloway

resolved to strangle her. But I had not provided anything for the purpose. I went downstairs and found the child at play with some cord. I asked for it and then got another small bit. I tied them together and then went upstairs for Celia.

Shortly after, we left the house together. We went through the streets with scarcely a word passing between us, until we came to the bottom of Edward Street. I desired her to stop there till I returned, saying I was going to call a mate of mine that lived there and he was going with us to the house where we were going to live. With that, I ran along to the house, and when I had seen Ann Kennett in the cupboard, I laid the small bit of cord on the window. Then I went to the door and waved my hand for Celia.

She came along and looked so innocent that I was ready to drop before she came to the door.

When she got there, I said my mate was not up yet and desired her to step in, for we would not wait for him; and I shut the door, pretending to hurry him.

When I came down, she — poor dear girl — was standing against the window where the fatal cord was lying. I went up to her and placed my arms round her neck, at the same time taking the cord in my hand. I fondled her as if I loved her. I kissed her several times: at the same time I tried to pass the cord round her neck, unobserved by her, as she stood by the window. But I could not succeed.

I then asked her to go and sit down on the stairs; which she did. I kept my arm around her neck, to prevent her seeing the cord as we moved from the window to the stairs. She sat down, and I sat down beside her. My heart was once or twice ready to fail; but I would not allow pity nor compassion to have any room in my breast. I sat with her some minutes, pretending to love her, and was on the point of giving up my purpose many times, and then I again took courage many times. At last I found I must either do it or give it up altogether.

The devil said: "Do it: it will not be discovered."

My keeping her there so long caused her, however, to suspect something not right. She looked at me very innocently and said: "How — how much longer will he be?" meaning the mate who, she thought, was above stairs.

The last words she ever spoke were: "Come, my dear, let us go."

These words were scarcely from her lips when, watching my opportunity, I, unknown to her, passed the cord round her neck.

It was then some minutes before I pulled it tight.

At last, I lost all natural feelings and pulled the cord with all my might. She never spoke nor groaned, but immediately sprang to her feet; but the attack was so sudden that she appeared not to have the power so much as to lift her hands to her neck.

I held her myself a few seconds; but the appearance of her face shocked me and, my arm beginning to ache, I called Ann Kennett. When she came out of the cupboard I desired her to come and assist me, which, God knows, she did, by taking hold of each end of the rope with me; and she held the rope with me until the poor girl dropped on the stairs.

We held her there until we judged that she was dead, and then Ann Kennett let go of the cord.

After that, I found that she was not dead.

Ann Kennett desired me not to let my heart fail me but to put
her [Celia] out of her misery as soon as possible. I dragged her
from the stairs to the middle of the kitchen. It would not do to let
her remain, for she began to revive. I then tied the cord as tight as I
was able, and then dragged her into the cupboard and hung her up
on some nails, so that she was then hanging by the neck.

Having at last accomplished the fell deed, Holloway took
Ann Kennett for a drink and then went home for a nap before
returning to the house with the intention of hiding the body in
Celia's own trunk. But although Celia was small, the trunk
was smaller, and so Holloway — who at one time had worked
as a butcher — set about cutting off the head and the limbs. (In
an especially macabre passage of the confession, he recalled
"taking off the legs at the knees without taking off the
stockings".)

Once the torso and thighs had been stowed in the trunk, and
the trunk wrapped round with Celia's spare outfit of clothes,
he parcelled up the head with the limbs and carried the
package to his lodgings in Margaret Street, near the sea-front,
where he undid the package and emptied it into the privy.

That night we went again to the house to wash away the blood,
which we did without much trouble: the floor being brick, the
blood never dried in as it might have done had it been boards.

The next day I borrowed a wheelbarrow, a pickaxe and a shovel
and took them down to the house. Then Ann Kennett met me at
the house at dusk. I put the trunk on the wheelbarrow and Kennett
took the pickaxe and shovel and came after me, just keeping in
sight of me. Although the night was beautifully bright, yet I felt, at
times, an involuntary shudder come over me when I looked at the
trunk that I was conveying to its place of secrecy.

Holloway had decided to bury the trunk in a copse beside
"Lover's Walk", a footpath near the village of Preston. One
can assume that he chose this location because of his intimate
knowledge of it. But here he again encountered problems:

I began to try to dig. I found it too dark: and what made it more
difficult were the roots of the trees, which were very thick.

"Holloway passing The Hare and Hounds to the copse at Lover's Walk."

Consequently I was obliged to drop the attempt for that time, and after putting the tools and the trunk in a place of security we returned home. . . .

On the following morning, as soon as it was light, we returned to the spot, intending to bury the trunk and all, but had not time to dig the hole deep enough. In my hurry, I took off the lid and turned it bottom uppermost, spilling the contents into the hole. I covered it over as soon as possible. I then broke the trunk into several pieces and threw most of it into the standing corn, while some I put under some bushes.

Still nothing went smoothly for Holloway. A week or so after the burial, a violent storm washed away the top covering of earth on the shallow grave, revealing part of Celia's dress, and some passers-by — one of them a Mr Sherlock — informed the High Constable of Preston. The *Brighton Gazette* reported:

As soon as the murder was confirmed, the copse was visited by a

179

great number of people from Brighton. . . . Some lace, said to
have been part of the cap, was picked up, and, with fragments of
the gown, was handed about and sold. To attempt to describe the
consternation which the knowledge of this event caused at
Brighton were a faint effort. Rumour, with its thousand tongues,
was busy to exaggerate every circumstance. . . .

During Sunday, the little village of Preston was crowded with
people visiting the copse and barn where the body was deposited.
Indeed, so eager were some persons, many of them females, to
view the body after it had been opened, that a hole was made in
the barn door. The effluvia made many of them regret their
curiosity.

Despite its incompleteness, the body was easily identified as
that of Celia Holloway by the diminutive proportions and the
clothing, which was recognized by Celia's mother. Ann
Kennett was arrested at once. Holloway, who had gone into
hiding, gave himself up after swallowing a rumour that the
body had been identified as that of another missing woman.

The evidence against him was formidable, and he was
committed to Horsham Gaol to await trial. There, having
added to his inefficiencies by making a hash of an attempt at
suicide, he "turned his face Zion-ward" and whiled away the
time by dictating confessions and writing sanctimonious,
moral-drawing epistles to relatives:

Deare Mother and Sister,

I, your unfortunate and unhappy son, once more out of prisson
take up my pen to right to you, hoping it may find you well, I
know not happy. I hope, my deare Mother you will not fail to pray
for me without ceasing, that God create in me a cleane heart, and
renew a right spirit with me, for now is the expected time, and
none but now is the day of Salvation.

I do not expect, dear mother, that you can send me anything but
I shall take it hard if my sister do not help me the few hours I have
to live, yet I know she will, for I know she loveth me.

Dear Mother and Sister,

I, your unfortunate son and brother do in·answer to your last
take up my pen to answer it as near as I can. I am very sorry to hear

"The Crown & Anchor at Preston, where the Coroner's Inquest was held, with the assembled multitude in consternation. Ann Kennett is sitting in the adjoining room."

that you should let this trouble you so much as to endanger your health, you ought to comfort yourself that the Lord hath dealt so mercifully toward me, to allow me so much time to make my peace with God.

Dear Mother,

You said you hoped that I would, for your sake , make a candid confession. Could I do anything more than what I have to convince you, and to appease offended justice, I would gladly do it; but as I have shook hands with the world, I cannot do anything to satisfy the curiosity of any man no further than what is consistent with divine justice. If the world will persist in judging the innocent I cannot help it, I have not failed to tell them that I am guilty, that I am the murderer; and if the innocent are judged let them bare with patience, but let those that judge them tremble at the following words spoken by Our Lord Himself:— "Judge not that ye be not judged!"

181

This last-quoted letter indicates that Holloway's mother was anxious to protect Ann Kennett — or, more likely, the baby that was now almost due. Subsequently, Holloway made what was probably the one chivalrous gesture of his life, ingeniously exculpating Ann Kennett by saying that he knew any number of women of that name and that the Ann Kennett mentioned in his early confessions was not necessarily the woman to whom he was bigamously married. Afterwards, however (as evidenced by the second paragraph of the following letter), his determination to be a martyr seems to have made him forgetful that the saving of Ann Kennett was his mother's idea.

> Dear Mother,
>
> I hope you will not be offended at what I am going to say, but to tell you the truth, I feel rather surprised that you said you was afraid you should lose your character and that you might as well lose your life. Have you forgot yourself or do you know against whom you speak, and do you not profess to trust in God? O my dear mother and sister, let not my punishment trouble you; for my soul's sake cease not to cry night and day that the Lord may receive my soul at last. Make it known to the minister of the Methodist Society that I desire an interest in all their prayers.
>
> I hope you don't think that because that poor innocent and unfortunate woman was living with me at the time, that I committed this, and on that and no other evidence she is to be accused. I tell you I have been the ruin of the girl, *and how can I seek to take away her life also.*

To reverse the proceedings, let me say that Ann Kennett, tried separately, was acquitted — more on account of the fact that she was big with child than that the prosecution was short of direct evidence — and that Holloway, tried at Lewes Assizes on 14 December, was found guilty. His execution, carried out two days later, was described thus by the *Brighton Gazette*:

> The hangman drew the cap over his eyes; and the chaplain continued to pray, concluding with the Lord's Prayer, during which Holloway, with great solemnity, repeatedly ejaculated, "Lord, receive my spirit," until the signal, when the bolt was

withdrawn, and the wretched culprit's life was at an end. He appeared to suffer but little. There was no manifestation of feeling in the crowd, nor could we perceive any tokens of commiseration.

Fifteen minutes or so after Holloway had been launched into eternity, a superstitious rustic from the village of Cowfold haggled with the hangman to have a wen, or cyst, on his forehead rubbed by the hanged man's hands; having reached a bargain, the hangman escorted the afflicted man on to the scaffold, undid the manacles and placed Holloway's hands on the wen. He kept them there for some time, while the rustic knelt, eyes closed, lips moving, body trembling; then, really giving value for money, he untied the man's kerchief and thrust it inside Holloway's shirt, proximate to the still heart, and in one deft movement transferred the kerchief to the wen. The treatment over, the man descended the steps — not without some difficulty, for he was holding the kerchief to his forehead with one hand, searching his purse for the hangman's fee with the other. Two women spectators, both with wens, pled for similar Laying On of Hands, but their transactions with the hangman were curtailed by the under-sheriff, who, worried that his breakfast was getting cold, ordered them to take themselves and their wens elsewhere.

The under-sheriff was understanding, though, about the hangman's traditional perk, and merely stood sighing impatiently while that worthy gave the rope that had hanged Holloway to a gentleman of Lewes in exchange for half-a-crown.

A Fabulous Monster

Anonymous[1]
(From a *Newgate Calendar*)

Sawney Beane was born in the county of East Lothian, about eight or nine miles eastward of the city of Edinburgh, some time in the reign of Queen Elizabeth, whilst King James I governed only in Scotland. His parents worked at hedging and ditching for their livelihood, and brought up their son to the same occupation. He got his daily bread in his youth by these means, but being very much prone to idleness, and not caring for being confined to any honest employment, he left his father and mother, and ran away into the desert part of the country, taking with him a woman as viciously inclined as himself. These two took up their habitation in a rock by the seaside, on a shore no great distance from Ballantrae, where they lived upwards of twenty-five years without going into any city, town or village.

In this time they had a great number of children and grandchildren, whom they brought up after their own manner, without any notions of humanity or civil society. They never kept any company but among themselves, and supported themselves wholly by robbing; being, moreover, so very cruel that they never robbed anyone whom they did not murder.

By this bloody method, and their living so retiredly from the world, they continued such a long time undiscovered, there being nobody able to guess how the people were lost that went by the place where they lived. As soon as they had robbed and murdered any man, woman or child, they used to carry off the carcass to the den, where, cutting it into quarters, they would

---

[1] EDITOR: Some bibliographers insist that this tale emerged from Scotch myth; that the protagonist is figmental. William Roughead favoured, "on grounds literary and artistic, an attribution to Defoe. . . . One would fain believe the Father of English Fiction to be the 'onlie begetter' of so remarkable an issue".

pickle the mangled limbs, and afterwards eat it; this being their only sustenance. And, notwithstanding they were at last so numerous, they commonly had superfluity of this their abominable food; so that in the night-time they frequently threw legs and arms of the unhappy wretches they had murdered into the sea, at a great distance from their bloody habitation. The limbs were often cast up by the tide in several parts of the country, to the astonishment and terror of all the beholders, and others who heard it. Persons who had gone about their lawful occasions fell so often into their hands that it caused a general outcry in the country round about, no man knowing what was become of his friend or relation, if they were once seen by these merciless cannibals.

All the people in the adjacent parts were at last alarmed at such a common loss of their neighbours and acquaintance; for there was no travelling in safety near the den of these wretches. This occasioned the sending of frequent spies into these parts, many of whom never returned again, and those who did, after the strictest search and inquiry, could not find how these melancholy matters happened. Several honest travellers were taken up on suspicion, and wrongfully hanged upon bare circumstances; several innocent innkeepers were executed for no other reason than that the persons who had been thus lost were known to have lain at their houses, which occasioned a suspicion of their being murdered by them and their bodies privately buried in obscure places to prevent discovery. Thus an ill-placed justice was executed with the greatest severity imaginable, in order to prevent these frequent atrocious deeds; so that not a few innkeepers, who lived on the Western Road of Scotland, left off their business, for fear of being made examples, and followed other employments. This on the other hand occasioned many great inconveniences to travellers, who were now in great distress for accommodation for themselves and their horses when they were disposed to bait, or put up for lodging at night. In a word, the whole country was almost depopulated.

Still the King's subjects were missing as much as before; so that it was the admiration of the whole kingdom how such villanies could be carried on and the villains not be found out. A great many had been executed, and not one of them all made any confession at the gallows, but stood to it at the last that they were perfectly innocent of the crimes for which they suffered. When the magistrates found all was in vain, they left off these rigorous proceedings, and trusted wholly to Providence for the bringing to light the authors of these unparalleled barbarities, when it should seem proper to the Divine wisdom.

Sawney's family was at last grown very large, and every branch of it, as soon as able, assisted in perpetrating their wicked deeds, which they still followed with impunity. Sometimes they would attack four, five or six footmen together, but never more than two if they were on horseback. They were, moreover, so careful that not one whom they set upon should escape, that an ambuscade was placed on every side to secure them, let them fly which way they would, provided it should ever so happen that one or more got away from the first assailants. How was it possible they should be detected, when not one that saw them ever saw anybody else afterwards? The place where they inhabited was quite solitary and lonesome; and when the tide came up, the water went for near two hundred yards into their subterraneous habitation, which reached almost a mile underground; so that when some who had been sent armed to search all the by-places about had passed by the mouth of their cave, they had never taken any notice of it, not supposing that anything human would reside in such a place of perpetual horror and darkness.

The number of people these savages destroyed was never exactly known, but it was generally computed that in the twenty-five years they continued their butcheries they had washed their hands in the blood of a thousand, at least, men, women and children. The manner how they were at last discovered was as follows.

A man and his wife behind him on the same horse coming one evening home from a fair, and falling into the ambuscade of these merciless wretches, they fell upon them in a most furious manner. The man, to save himself as well as he could,

Sawney Beane at the entrance of his cave

fought very bravely against them with sword and pistol, riding some of them down, by main force of his horse. In the conflict the poor woman fell from behind him, and was instantly murdered before her husband's face; for the female cannibals cut her throat and fell to sucking her blood with as great a gusto as if it had been wine. This done, they ripped up her belly and pulled out all her entrails. Such a dreadful spectacle made the man make the more obstinate resistance, as expecting the same fate if he fell into their hands. It pleased Providence, while he was engaged, that twenty or thirty from the same fair came together in a body; upon which Sawney Beane and his bloodthirsty clan withdrew, and made the best of their way through a thick wood to their den.

This man, who was the first that had ever fallen in their way and come off alive, told the whole company what had happened, and showed them the horrid spectacle of his wife, whom the murderers had dragged to some distance, but had not time to carry her entirely off. They were all struck with stupefaction and amazement at what he related, took him with them to Glasgow, and told the affair to the provost of that city, who immediately sent to the King concerning it.

In about three or four days after, his Majesty himself in person, with a body of about four hundred men, set out for the place where this dismal tragedy was acted, in order to search all the rocks and thickets, that, if possible, they might apprehend this hellish curse, which had been so long pernicious to all the western parts of the kingdom.

The man who had been attacked was the guide, and care was taken to have a large number of bloodhounds with them, that no human means might be wanting towards their putting an entire end to these cruelties.

No sign of any habitation was to be found for a long time, and even when they came to the wretches' cave they took no notice of it, but were going to pursue their search along the seashore, the tide being then out. But some of the bloodhounds luckily entered this Cimmerian den, and instantly set up a most hideous barking, howling and yelping; so that the King, with his attendants, came back and looked into it. They could not

189

yet tell how to conceive that anything human could be concealed in a place where they saw nothing but darkness. Nevertheless, as the bloodhounds increased their noise, went farther in, and refused to come back again, they began to imagine there was some reason more than ordinary. Torches were now immediately sent for, and a great many men ventured in through the most intricate turnings and windings, till at last they arrived at that private recess from all the world which was the habitation of these monsters.

Now the whole body, or as many of them as could, went in, and were all so shocked at what they beheld that they were almost ready to sink into the earth. Legs, arms, thighs, hands and feet of men, women and children were hung up in rows, like dried beef. A great many limbs lay in pickle, and a great mass of money, both gold and silver, with watches, rings, swords, pistols, and a large quantity of clothes, both linen and woollen, and an infinite number of other things, which they had taken from those whom they had murdered, were thrown together in heaps, or hung up against the sides of the den.

Sawney's family at this time, besides him, consisted of his wife, eight sons, six daughters, eighteen grandsons, and fourteen granddaughters, who were all begotten in incest.

These were all seized and pinioned by his Majesty's order in the first place; then they took what human flesh they found and buried it in the sands; afterwards loading themselves with the spoils which they found, they returned to Edinburgh with their prisoners, all the country, as they passed along, flocking to see this cursed tribe. When they were come to their journey's end, the wretches were all committed to the Tollbooth, whence they were the next day conducted under a strong guard to Leith, where they were all executed without any process, it being thought needless to try creatures who were such professed enemies to mankind.

The men had their hands and legs severed from their bodies; by which amputations they bled to death in some hours. The wife, daughters and grandchildren, having been made spectators of this just punishment inflicted on the men, were afterwards burnt to death in three several fires. They all in

general died without the least signs of repentance, but
continued cursing and venting the most dreadful imprecations
to the very last gasp of life.

Acknowledgements and Sources

"The Murder on Yarmouth Sands": from *Great Stories of Real Life*, edited by Max Pemberton, London, n.d. "The Wearmouth Murder": from *The Chronicles of Crime; or The New Newgate Calendar. Being a Series of Memoirs and Anecdotes of Notorious Characters who have outraged the Laws of Great Britain from the Earliest Period to 1841*, edited by Camden Pelham, London, 1887. "The Late Irene Munro": from *Posts-Mortem: The Correspondence of Murder*, Newton Abbot, 1971. "The Shooting at Stella Maris": from *The Life of Sir Edward Marshall Hall*, London, 1930. "Angels of Death": by permission of the author. "Also Known as Love": a version of an article published in the *Manchester Evening News*, by permission of the author. "The Secret of Ireland's Eye": from *The Art of Murder*, New York, 1943; by permission of Marjorie Roughead. "The Poisoned Chocolates": from *Murders and Murder Trials, 1812–1912*, London, 1922. "Matricide at the Metropole": an article first published in *Police Review*, by permission of the author. "The Bones of Brandy Cove": by permission of the author. "The Podmore Case": from *Crime and Its Detection*, edited by W. Teignmouth Shore, London, 1931. "The First Trunk Murder": an article first published in *Police Review*, by permission of the author. "A Fabulous Monster": from *The Complete Newgate Calendar. Being Captain Charles Johnson's General History of the Lives and Adventures of the Most Famous Highwaymen, Murderers, Street-Robbers and Account of the Voyages and Plunders of the Most Notorious Pyrates, 1734; Captain Alexander Smith's Compleat History of the Lives and Robberies of the Most Notorious Highwayman, Foot-Pads, Shop-Lifts and Cheats, 1719; The Tyburn Chronicle, 1768; The Malefactors' Register, 1796; George Borrow's Celebrated Trials, 1825; The Newgate Calendar, by Andrew Knapp and William Baldwin, 1826; Camden Pelham's Chronicles of Crime, 1841; etc.*, collated and edited by G. T. Crook, London, 1926.